Crossroads

Choosing the Road to Sexual Purity

Facilitator's Guide

By: David Longacre
    Small group format adaptation by Dan Strickland

Communications should be addressed to:

Turning Point Ministries	**or**	Harvest USA
P. O. Box 221217		P. O. Box 11469
Chattanooga, TN 37422-2127		Philadelphia, PA 19111
www.turningpointministries.org		www.harvestusa.org

Scripture quotations marked (NIV) are taken from the *Holy Bible*, NEW INTERNATIONAL VERSION®. Copyright © 1973, 1978, 1984 International Bible Society. All rights reserved throughout the world. Used by permission of International Bible Society.

Scripture quotations marked (NASB) are taken from the *New American Standard Bible*®, Copyright © 1960, 1962, 1963, 1968, 1971, 1972, 1973, 1975, 1977, 1995 by The Lockman Foundation. Used by permission. (www.Lockman.org)

Scripture quotations marked (NLT) are taken from the *Holy Bible*, New Living Translation, copyright © 1996. Used by permission of Tyndale House Publishers, Inc., Wheaton, Illinois 60189. All rights reserved.

Scripture quotations marked (NKJV) are taken from the New King James Version. Copyright © 1982 by Thomas Nelson, Inc. Used by permission.

ISBN 1-58119-049-2

Layout: Louise Lee
Cover Photo:www.comstock.com

About the Author

David E. Longacre is on the staff of Harvest USA and oversees small group ministry for men who struggle with sexual sins such as pornography, fantasy, masturbation, physical adultery, and prostitution. He also leads seminars and teaches on the subject of sexual sin. An ordained pastor in the Presbyterian Church in America, he has served three churches in Pennsylvania, Tennessee, and New Jersey over a 17-year period. First discovering pornography at age 13, David understands the rollercoaster ride of sexual addiction and the dynamics of trying to live a double life. He has been involved with the groups at Harvest USA since 1994, has served as a volunteer and as a part-time staff member, and has been a full-time staff member since 2000. David has a bachelor of arts from Eastern College, a master of divinity from Princeton Theological Seminary, and is working toward a master of Christian counseling at Philadelphia Biblical University.

About the Small Group Editor

Dan T. Strickland has served as vice president of Turning Point Ministries since 1992 and has trained many churches in the United States and other countries to implement Turning Point groups. He has 17 years pastoral experience, most recently as adult pastor and counselor in a congregation that used Turning Point groups to reach hundreds of participants in the church, community, and jails. He has authored the small group curriculum, *Completely Free!*, facilitated the demonstration group in the *Living Free* training series, and adapted the content of the *Living Free* manuals to coordinate with the video segments. He is a graduate of Central Bible College and Southwestern Baptist Theological Seminary, where he earned a master of divinity.

Crossroads
Choosing the Road to Sexual Purity

Contents

Preface

Harvest USA and Turning Point Ministries have joined together to produce this small group curriculum—*Crossroads: Choosing the Road to Sexual Purity*. This small group bible study is based on materials the author has used for years in providing support and accountability groups for those struggling with sexual brokenness and sin. This group is part of a group of small group curriculums developed by Turning Point Ministries whose mission is to equip churches and ministries to help people turn to God and his resources when struggling with life's problems. Information about leading Turning Point small groups can be found in our training series, *Living Free*, and in the *Core Team Manual* and *Small Group Skills Guide* published by Turning Point Ministries. More information about small group resources and leadership is available at www.turningpointministries.org. More information about dealing with and helping people struggling with sexual sin is available at www.harvestusa.org.

One thing to keep in mind is to avoid labeling this group as one only for sex addicts. Everyone will benefit from participating in this group because the materials are just as useful for those who desire to continue to walk in purity as they are for those who are already trapped and looking for a way out. Because sexual sins occur most often in secret, it is easy for people who have these problems to hide. The truth is that there are many people in your church or ministry who are struggling in secret with these problems. By not stigmatizing the group, you will make it easier for many more to find the help they need.

Facilitating a group like this is guaranteed to stretch you spiritually. In a society that celebrates sexual sin, you will be leading a group for people who want to celebrate holiness and escape the deception and temptation of a world enslaved by sexual sin. You will be pointing group members (as well as yourself) to a deeper relationship with Jesus as the one who can salvage broken lives and lead us out of the confusion of a society gone mad. Group members are choosing the road to sexual purity, but the road is not an easy road and some will face detours and breakdowns along the way. That is why your involvement is so important. You will be the personal, caring voice that encourages people to continue their journey out of brokenness and sin.

Facilitating a Crossroads group is not something you should do alone. You will need the inspiration and accountability of at least one other person. Ideally, you will be part of larger group of people who lead other groups. This will give you someone with whom you can pray, talk about the group, share concerns, strategize, and just vent when you feel frustrated.

Group facilitators do not have to have a personal history with compulsive sexual sin. It is important, however, that facilitators be aware that they are "limping leaders"—that is, that they are aware of their own sin and brokenness before God and are leading the group from a humble awareness of their own weaknesses. If you are aware of your own struggles with sin and are willing to admit them, you are in a position to be compassionate to those who are losing their battles with sin.

Your job is not to be a counselor. We are not about counseling in these groups. We are seeking to do what Jesus calls us to do—to make disciples by helping others walk in repentance and faith. The most important qualification you need to facilitate this group is Christian maturity and a solid, daily walk with God. Leaders should be accountable to a church or ministry that endorses the group meeting.

The focus of the group needs to be how Christ is working in our lives. Participants need to be able to talk about their struggles, but if the struggles become the focus, then the group will become discouraged. We know God is at work in the lives of believers, so always keep the main focus on the here and now and how God is at work to take us from where we are to where he wants us to be.

There are some people who are not good candidates for this group and would probably be a hindrance to other members. Discourage attendance by those who:
- Are openly and verbally hostile to the gospel and the Christian message.
- Are not interested in lasting change.
- Have extreme chemical addiction issues that need to be addressed first.
- Are currently involved in illegal activities such as pimping, sexual abuse, child pornography, etc.
- Have deeper emotional issues than the group is designed to address.
- Are going only to please someone else or to avoid legal consequences.

The group needs to understand the importance of confidentiality. Anything that is said within the group should stay within the group. If confidence is violated, it can destroy the group. There are some exceptions to confidentiality that should be mentioned to everyone before the group begins. Most states have mandatory reporting laws if an adult admits to sexual activity with a minor. You should check with the authorities or a legal professional about the law in your area. Also, if someone is threatening to harm himself or herself or another person, the group should know that confidence will be broken. Facilitators should contact the minister or elders of the church if any of the above situations occur, and they should together seek appropriate professional guidance. Make it a priority to have a relationship with those who can offer legal, medical, and psychological advice. You may never need it; but if you do, you will want to act quickly.

The leadership you are providing the group cannot be underestimated. To make the group as good as possible, watch out for these common pitfalls:
- Do not have coed groups. Men and women should meet in separate groups.
- Do not allow the group to become a gripe session where participants blame others and take on a victim mentality.
- Do not allow the group to feel superior to other Christians just because they are willing to admit their sins.
- Do not allow a group member to dominate the group's time by becoming the center of attention week after week or by allowing them to tell their story over and over.
- Do not allow any of the group members to become the problem solvers for other group members. Some will concentrate on solving the problems of others to avoid dealing with their own issues.
- Advise participants to be careful about friendships within the group. When sharing personal issues, strong bonds can occur between people. It is important that participants encourage one another to grow in Christ and not be a source of temptation.
- Be aware that there may be "predators" in the group who are looking to prey upon the weaker members.

Finally, remember this: Your involvement is important. Never forget: It is not your responsibility to change people. God brings the change when people look to him for help. When this group is complete, you will have many memories of how God's transforming grace worked in members' lives.

Getting Started

Group Size

We suggest that each *Crossroads* group have two group leaders (facilitators) and a maximum of 12 participants. Having more than 12 may prevent some from being a part of much-needed discussion.

Preparation Time

The facilitator's material is written in an almost word-for-word dialogue. However, it is hoped that as you come to know and understand the concepts presented, you will be able to "personalize" each session to better fit your own style. Highlight the points you want to emphasize and make notes for yourself.

Your group is unique—so adapt questions to their needs and situations. Be sensitive to each person who is in your group.

Keep in mind that the answers provided for the discussion questions are there only as a tool to assist you and may not be the only "right" answers to the questions being asked.

Become thoroughly familiar with the four elements of each session:
- Introduction
- Self-Awareness
- Spiritual Awareness
- Application

You will find more detail about these on the following page.

The facilitators should meet prior to each session to pray and make final plans. They should also meet briefly after each session to discuss what happened during the meeting and go over any follow-up that may be needed.

Crossroads Group Member Guides

Before Session 1, the *Crossroads* group member guides should be distributed to each group member. Facilitators should be thoroughly familiar with the material before the first meeting.

Encourage group members to complete the appropriate assignments prior to each group meeting. Through the readings and other exercises in the group member guide, group members can come to each session better prepared for meaningful discussion.

Correlation Between Facilitator's Guide and Group Member's Guide

Facilitator's Guide — This guide is designed to lead the group through the four-phase small group format. The facilitator's responsibility is to start the discussion, give it direction, and thereafter simply keep the discussion personal and on track.

The text is presented in the left column. The right column contains tips and pointers for leading the group along with answers to questions. The facilitator will prayerfully present select questions because there are usually more questions than time permits.

Although the text is presented in the Group Member's Guide, it may not in some cases be word for word as in the Facilitator's Guide. For example, the Introductions are different in the two guides. The Facilitator's Guide is directed toward opening prayer and a go-around question; whereas, the Group Member's Guide focuses on devotions for the week which is a part of preparation for the upcoming session.

Group Member's Guide — This guide is designed to be done as homework, preparing the participant for meaningful ministry during the small group session. Although the general text is the same as Self-Awareness, Spiritual Awareness, and Application in the Facilitator's Guide, concentration should be on the group process during the actual group experience.

It is good for the participant to bring the Group Member's Guide to the group session; however, the participant should be more attentive to the group process rather than trying to find text or written answers in the Group Member's Guide. Each group member should bring a Bible for meaningful study and application of God's Word for daily living.

In a Nutshell — The Facilitator's Guide is designed to lead the group process through *Crossroads*. The Group Member's Guide will prepare the participant for the group meeting.

Suggested Group Format

The group format for each session consists of four elements: Introduction, Self-Awareness, Spiritual Awareness, and Application. There is a reason for each phase. The facilitators should always plan each session with this format in mind.

Part I Introduction
(10 minutes)

Begin with prayer. The facilitator may pray or may ask one of the group members to lead in prayer. After the prayer, a sharing question helps put the group at ease and makes the members more comfortable in being a part of the discussion. The lead facilitator should respond to the sharing question first, followed by the co-facilitator. This helps the group members to feel safer in participating in the exercise. After the facilitators have shared, the group members will share one after another around the circle. Always remind group members they are not expected to share if they do not wish to do so. The rule is that everyone works within his or her comfort level and is welcome to pass.

This is not the time for detailed conversation, so ask the members of the group to keep their comments brief. If a person is obviously in pain during the exercise, the facilitator should interrupt the sharing and pray for the person in pain. After prayer, the exercise may resume.

Part II Self-Awareness
(20-25 minutes)

After the sharing question, the facilitator will lead the group into the Self-Awareness phase. Self-Awareness is a time to discuss the practical issues involved in *Crossroads*. It is important to stay on the subject matter. This is a time to focus on needs and healing, not to have a "martyr" or "pity party."

It is suggested in Self-Awareness that the facilitators ask the group members to share as they wish rather than going around the circle as in the Introduction phase. This is because people are at various comfort levels, and they should not feel pressured to self-disclose if they are uncomfortable. As the group continues to meet, members will feel more and more comfortable in being a part of the discussion.

Remember, prayer is always in order. If a group member is hurting during this phase, stop and pray. One of the facilitators may lead in prayer or ask another group member to pray. This says to the group members that each one is important and that you care about each individual.

Part III Spiritual Awareness
(20-25 minutes)

After the Self-Awareness phase, the facilitator will lead the group into the bible study time. Having briefly explained the topic, the facilitator should assign Scriptures listed in the Facilitator's Guide to group members. When each Scripture is called by the facilitator, the group member should read the verse(s). After the verses are read, give time for discussion.

Part IV Application
(20 minutes)

This part is actually a continuation of Part III. Ask for volunteers to share their reflections on the question. The facilitators should emphasize the importance of the group members' applying biblical principles to their lives. Help begins with right thinking. The Bible says, "Be transformed by the renewing of your mind" (Romans 12:2 NIV). Obedience to the Word should follow with right behavior. Right feelings will follow right thinking and right behavior.

Facilitator's Guide: *Crossroads*, Turning Point, P. O. Box 22127, Chattanooga, TN 37422-2127

Session 1 *Sexual Sin as Slavery*

Introduction

Allow 10 Minutes

Opening Prayer

> Ask God to show group members the extent to which sin has bound them and the promise of freedom that comes through Christ.

Sharing Questions

Ask group members to introduce themselves and give two facts about themselves.

> Personal response

Self-Awareness

Allow 20-25 Minutes

> NOTE TO FACILITATOR:
>
> This lesson contains a great amount of information, and you may not be able to cover all of it in the time you have. Be alert to going too long in discussing the cycle. If you run out of time, bridge right into the sharing time as you see the link between the cycle and what the participants are experiencing at the moment. This lesson forms the basis for the rest of the lessons, but it is not essential that everything be covered for the rest of the lessons to make sense. Keep the "Sin System" in the back of your mind throughout the rest of the lessons as it gives a model to quickly target where people may be in their struggles. A familiarity with the cycle allows both the facilitator and the participants to quickly locate what might be going on in their hearts and behavior.

The Bible states clearly that when we are involved in sinful behaviors, we are entering a process of becoming enslaved to the sin. While this slavery may not be noticeable at first, it is like the deepening of dusk. As the sun begins to set, we do not see the change in the light—especially if it is a cloudy day. Slowly the twilight grows and imperceptibly the evening comes. At first we do not notice it at all, but as it gets darker and darker, we realize that night is descending. Suddenly it truly is dark, and we have failed to seek the shelter of our father's home. We suddenly know that we are wandering about in pitch-black darkness with no hope.

Sin grows this way: slowly but surely. Psalm 101:3 warns us that if we look on sinful things, they can reach out and get a grip on us. "I will set no worthless thing before my eyes; I hate the work of those who fall away; It shall not fasten its grip on me" (NASB).

In an age before the printing press and camera, this verse illustrates the dangers of pornography. King David knew that if he looked upon the activities of sin—the prostitution in the foreign temples of the false god Baal—he could be lured and trapped by it. We can know this same truth today. Pornography and all the related "adult" businesses appeal to the eye and through the eye to the heart. Those who look upon sinful things can expect that those things will reach out and grasp them. God warns us that slavery to sin is the inevitable consequence of our sin. A careful reading of Proverbs 5-7 reveals the real danger of sexual immorality. The man involved in it is ultimately described as one who is like an ox going to the slaughter, a prisoner in chains, a bird in a snare, and someone with an arrow stuck in his liver! What stronger images can we find of slavery and death?

Is it any surprise that our experience seems like one of bondage? Is it any surprise to hear someone say, "I don't know why I keep doing this! I can't control myself!" or "It is like the car turns itself into the parking lot of the strip joint!" or "Once I'm online, I cannot help but go to the porn sites and the chatrooms!"

In modern terminology, we call behavior that seems out of our control an "addiction." This word can be used by some as an excuse to avoid responsibility. We use this word to describe a bondage-like slavery to a behavior, but this bondage does not excuse our personal responsibility for our actions. When we refer to someone as being a sex addict, we mean that he or she is so absorbed by out-of-control sexual behavior that life is unmanageable.

In his book, *Contrary to Love*, Dr. Patrick Carnes identified a typical cycle of behavior through which individuals who are sexually addicted go. Though his model does not come out of an interpretation of the Bible, there appears to be nothing in his description that would contradict the Bible.

On page 10 is "The Carnes Model of Sexual Addiction" to which we have added pertinent Bible verses and renamed "The Sin System." You will want to refer to this diagram as we go through the following concepts. This lesson will focus on this cycle, how we can identify where we are in it, and what we can do—by God's grace—to get out of it.

The Carnes model begins with a faulty belief system that leads to impaired thinking (Figure 1).

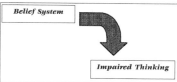

Figure 1

The Carnes model proposes that the core belief system of a sexually addicted person is not based upon reality and that this distorted belief system is central to the addiction process. Persons bound by sexual sin have a negative self-image, do not believe that others would care for them if they really knew them, and believe that sex is their most important need because sex makes life bearable.

People with a faulty belief system will have a distorted view of reality because of their impaired thinking based on their false belief system. Addicted people so hate themselves that they try to cover the shame by rationalization and lies. But because they recognize their attempts as self-deception, they isolate themselves so that no one will confront them with the truth and upset their world where they excuse themselves and blame others. This whole chain of events causes the person to identify himself or herself as a depraved and hopeless sinner, beyond even the grace of God, thus reinforcing the faulty belief system.

This impaired thinking opens the door to an addictive cycle shown in the sin system diagram as the behavioral subcycle.

The flawed core beliefs and the process of delusion work together to fuel the addiction that Dr. Carnes describes as a four-phase process. These phases are: preoccupation, ritualization, sexual compulsiveness, and despair (Figure 2).

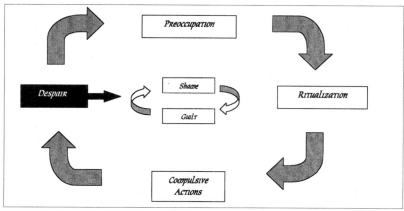

Figure 2

- **Preoccupation**

The person becomes obsessed with sexual stimulation, thinks about it all the time, and enters a trance-like state when contemplating being sexual.

Are there any situations, circumstances, or even people who "trigger" the cycle in you? (In other words, what kinds of things cause you to become preoccupied and move towards your ritual and sin?)

This will vary, but note that certain stress-related patterns will emerge in the discussion. Also note that perceptions of the opposite sex and parents may fit in here.

- **Ritualization**

The person goes through routines when contemplating sexual experience which intensify the trance-like state and heighten arousal and excitement.

Identify as many parts of your "ritual" as possible.

If no one is able to identify his ritual, then discuss how some people's rituals involve which route home they take from work. Someone may wear a particular T-shirt which does not have any Christian symbols on it when contemplating a sexual encounter later in the day. Another may have a particular path through the mall to get to the bookstore or to walk past a lingerie store. Realize that rituals are not always obvious to others.

- **Sexual Compulsiveness**

This is a seemingly overwhelming compulsion to act out sexually with no regard to possible negative consequences.

- **Despair**

This is the hopelessness that comes from feeling powerless to control the sexual compulsion that is driving the person to destruction.

This is the condition described in Proverbs 5:22: "His own iniquities will capture the wicked, and he will be held with the cords of his sin" (NASB).

Have you ever thought about the relationship of shame to preoccupation? How do unresolved guilt feelings and the shame that accompanies them actually push you back into the cycle?

Focus on the fact that the guilt is often used to push the cycle forward. Satan will tempt us with this lie: "You might as well go do it since you already have shown you can't resist. You are nothing but a sinner, so go do it. You know you liked it. It will make you feel better."

The addicted person's life becomes unmanageable while struggling to manage two lives: the public life and the addicted life. The previous four phases form a behavioral loop, a vicious circle that intensifies the guilt, shame, pain, and fear each time the person goes through them. In order to manage these negative feelings, the addicted person seeks to find comfort once again in compulsive sexual behavior.

In what ways do you see this *cycle* occurring in your life right now?

> This question may raise a variety of responses, depending on the present situation of the group participants. Allow the participants to describe what is going on in their lives. This can be recalled during the sharing and prayer request time of the group meeting.

What part of the cycle seems to be the worst for you?

> This also may vary. For some participants, it is the guilt and shame section; for others, it is the struggle of preoccupation followed by the ritualization that they feel helpless against.

Spiritual Awareness Lead–In

Jesus answered them, "Truly, truly, I say to you, everyone who commits sin is the slave of sin" (John 8:34, NASB).

Jesus teaches that those who continue habitually in the same sin are said to be slaves of sin.

Do you think this is too strong a word to describe a person caught in a cycle of sin? Why or why not?

> Answers will vary.

Spiritual-Awareness

Allow 20-25 Minutes

The model of the sexual addiction process Dr. Carnes describes is just that—only a model that attempts to illustrate the process of sexual addiction. We will use this model to illustrate the process and to show where biblical insights can help a person break free from this vicious cycle of self-destruction.

Following is an adaptation of Dr. Carnes' model to illustrate what we will refer to as "The Sin System."

The Sin System

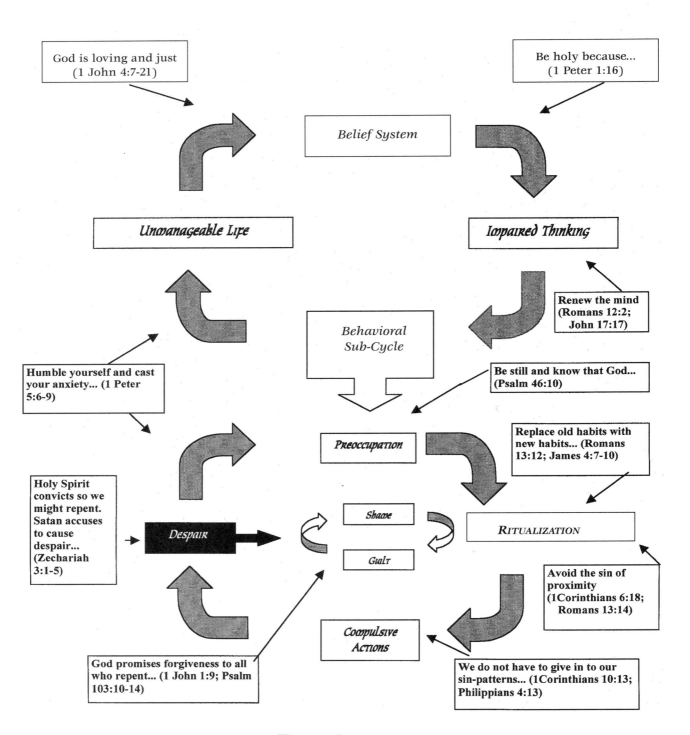

Figure 3

Adapted from *Contrary to Love* by Patrick Carnes.
Copyright 1989 by Hazelden Foundation.
Reprinted by permission of Hazelden Foundation, Center City, Minn.

The first thing to notice in this diagram is that the cycle begins with a belief system through which we determine what is right and wrong and evaluate our thoughts and actions. It is the framework we use to make decisions and live our lives.

A healthy belief system judges what is right and wrong in view of the Scriptures, but a faulty belief system has no true moral anchor. Out of a healthy belief system flows a healthy respect of God, self, and others. An addicted person's belief system is self-centered and produces a life that dishonors God, disgraces self, and disrespects others. Sexually addicted people believe that sex is their most important need and this belief influences the choices they make.

The second step is the impaired thinking that comes as a result of denying the truth about our actions. As a person denies that certain actions are wrong, he or she will become more deluded and confused. The addicted person ignores the mounting consequences of sinful behaviors and refuses to change even though the pain resulting from a sinful lifestyle is constantly increasing. The person becomes more confused while entering into a defensive lifestyle where rationalizing sin, blaming others, and other attempts of self-deception make it easier to choose to act out sexually (as described in the behavioral subcycle).

The behavioral subcycle intensifies the addiction and results in the next stage where life is unmanageable. Important areas of life decline, and the addiction costs us something we love. It may be our family, job, reputation, self-respect—whatever it may be, the pain of an unmanageable life pushes an addicted person back into the belief system where the false idea that sex is the most important thing in life launches the process all over again.

If it is true, as Dr. Carnes suggests, that an addicted person's core beliefs motivate him or her toward sinful acting out, what plan would you suggest to change those core beliefs?

False beliefs can become so strong that they define who we are and have to be relentlessly exposed to the truth until the truth replaces the lies that we believe.

One of the most persistent false beliefs is that we will always be trapped and there is no hope for us. God, however, has a different point of view.

Galatians 5:1

> It was for freedom that Christ set us free; therefore keep standing firm and do not be subject again to a yoke of slavery. (*NASB*)

Take another look at the Sin System diagram, paying attention to the biblical references shown. Do any of the Bible verses listed on the chart stand out to you as you consider at what point you find yourself in this model of "The Sin System"?

What hope do you find in them?

Personal responses.

Luke 4:18-21

As Jesus began his ministry, he read the following quotation from the prophet Isaiah to the congregation he was addressing.

> "The Spirit of the Lord is upon me, for he has appointed me to preach Good News to the poor. He has sent me to proclaim that captives will be released, that the blind will see, that the downtrodden will be freed from their oppressors, and that the time of the Lord's favor has come."

> He rolled up the scroll, handed it back to the attendant, and sat down. Everyone in the synagogue stared at him intently. Then he said, "This Scripture has come true today before your very eyes!" (NLT)

If you had been sitting in that congregation, in what areas would you want to ask Jesus to help you?

Personal responses.

Most people who are sexually addicted live in such a state of guilt and shame that they believe they are defective, that they can never change, and that nobody who really knows who they are would love them. This hopelessness drives them deeper into their sin. The truth is that God loves us, even when we are doing what is wrong.

Romans 5:6-8

> When we were utterly helpless, Christ came at just the right time and died for us sinners. Now, no one is likely to die for a good person, though someone might be willing to die for a person who is especially good. But God showed his great love for us by sending Christ to die for us while we were still sinners. (NLT)

How difficult do you find it to believe that God could love you, even as you find yourself feeling helpless to change? Would you love someone like yourself? Would you die in someone's place who was just like you?

Answers will vary, but encourage participants to try to understand the concept that God loves those whom we consider to be the unlovable.

It is the death of Jesus in our place, the payment of the debt we owe God for our disobedience, that makes it possible for us to change and be a person whose lifestyle pleases him. Some people suffer the pain of their condition for decades before finding help, just as the woman described in the following passage suffered 18 years.

Facilitator's Guide: *Crossroads*, Turning Point, P. O. Box 22127, Chattanooga, TN 37422-2127

Luke 13:10-13

One Sabbath day as Jesus was teaching in a synagogue, he saw a woman who had been crippled by an evil spirit. She had been bent double for eighteen years and was unable to stand up straight. When Jesus saw her, he called her over and said, "Woman, you are healed of your sickness!" Then he touched her, and instantly she could stand straight. How she praised and thanked God! (NLT)

What was the condition of the woman and how long had she had this condition? What was causing the condition?

> She had been bent over double for 18 years. This was a condition caused by a demon. It was a physical manifestation of a spiritual problem.

Who initiated the healing of the woman?

> Jesus

Why is Jesus able to heal those bound by spirits and give release?

> He is God!

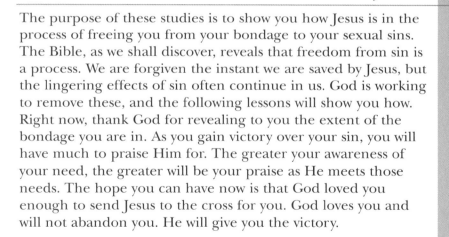

Application

The purpose of these studies is to show you how Jesus is in the process of freeing you from your bondage to your sexual sins. The Bible, as we shall discover, reveals that freedom from sin is a process. We are forgiven the instant we are saved by Jesus, but the lingering effects of sin often continue in us. God is working to remove these, and the following lessons will show you how. Right now, thank God for revealing to you the extent of the bondage you are in. As you gain victory over your sin, you will have much to praise Him for. The greater your awareness of your need, the greater will be your praise as He meets those needs. The hope you can have now is that God loved you enough to send Jesus to the cross for you. God loves you and will not abandon you. He will give you the victory.

If you could know that God loves you just as you are and offers you a chance for forgiveness, how do you think it would change the dynamic of the Sin System in your life?

> If you do not experience forgiveness, then you might as well continue in your sin. Without forgiveness, there is no hope of eternal life; and without that, there is no reason to resist temptation. Only forgiveness can break this part of the cycle and prevent individuals from looping back around.

Closing Prayer

> Pray for any specific needs group members may express. Pray for encouragement and wisdom for the group.

Introduction

Allow 10 Minutes

Opening Prayer

Pray that group members will be able to understand the impact of lust on our spiritual lives.

Sharing Questions
Ask group members to share if understanding "The Sin System" has helped them since the last session. If so, how?

Personal response.

Self-Awareness

Allow 20-25 Minutes

NOTE TO FACILITATOR:

It is important to realize that individuals struggling with sexual sins have a hard time being objective about this subject. There may be a great deal of shame and guilt clouding their ability to read the Bible objectively. (Also note that in 99.9 percent of the cases of masturbation, lust is present; therefore, it is pretty safe to assume that masturbation involves sin.)

Any discussion of the subject of masturbation is sure to generate strong opinions and emotions. Because most people begin dealing with this issue in adolescence and for many it becomes the first experience of the sin cycle (preoccupation, ritualization, compulsive action, despair), it is always going to be an emotional issue. Some are convinced that masturbation is 100 percent—always—a sin, while others believe it is their only way to release sexual tension and is certainly better than other options. Everyone seems to have an opinion.

Facilitator's Guide: *Crossroads*, Turning Point, P. O. Box 22127, Chattanooga, TN 37422-2127

In the end, the only opinion that really matters is God's opinion. That is why it is so important to base our thinking on what the Bible specifically says about masturbation. The problem lies in the fact that the Bible does not use the word "masturbation" and never deals with the subject directly. A few passages can be used to shed some light on the subject, but these involve circumstances that have frequently been misunderstood and misinterpreted. Because of this confusion, Christians tend to fall into two extreme positions: (1) masturbation is always a sin, and (2) masturbation is not a sin.

In order to discuss this topic without immediately dividing into these two positions, we want to ask, "Is masturbation always wrong?" Considering the topic in this way will help us to consider a broad biblical perspective.

In your religious training, was masturbation discussed as a healthy expression of sexuality or as a sinful behavior?

Personal responses.

Was there any middle position taught?

Personal responses.

What did you believe?

Personal responses.

There is an argument that states that since practically everyone masturbates—or has masturbated at some time in his or her life—the behavior is to be looked at as normal and possibly as a necessary and healthy part of sexual development. This view often states that so long as someone is not doing it frequently and habitually, then it is harmless and may be even something to seek after for occasional release of sexual tension. This argument is based on the argument that "Everyone is doing it."

What other behaviors can be justified by the phrase, "Everyone is doing it"?

Cheating, stealing, being promiscuous, using drugs illegally, etc.

The problem with this line of reasoning is that the Bible states that everyone is sinful. It is possible that masturbation is a sinful manifestation of our sinful natures and maybe it is a universal sin which points to the universal sinfulness of humanity, just like selfishness and unrighteous anger. However, just because something is universal does not mean that it is sinful. Everyone is selfish. Everyone has been less than respectful to his or her parents at least once. Everyone eats. Everyone sleeps. Unless something is specifically identified in the Bible as sin or can be clearly shown as an act or attitude rooted in something that is a sin, we cannot know for sure if it is a sin. Such is the problem with the question of masturbation.

Spiritual Awareness Lead-In

As we have discussed, masturbation is considered by some to be a natural behavior common to every human.

Is there a difference between what is natural behavior for every human and what should be normal behavior for a Christian? What makes the difference?

Human beings in our natural state have been corrupted by sin so that what comes naturally to us is in opposition to God's will. We act to please ourselves. When we are born again, we become a new creation, and God's Spirit gives us the ability to lead a life that pleases God. This lifestyle is very different from the lifestyle that comes naturally to us.

Spiritual-Awareness

Allow 20-25 Minutes

In an effort to understand this issue, we need to look at a series of biblical references that many people think address the issue of masturbation. As mentioned earlier, the Bible does not directly deal with the subject, but that does not mean it has nothing to say about the matter.

Some people use the story of the "sin of Onan" to argue that masturbation is always sinful. The following passage will give the background information needed to understand the story of Onan.

Have the group read Deuteronomy 25:5-10.

Deuteronomy 25:5-10

> If brothers are living together and one of them dies without a son, his widow must not marry outside the family. Her husband's brother shall take her and marry her and fulfill the duty of a brother-in-law to her. The first son she bears shall carry on the name of the dead brother so that his name will not be blotted out from Israel.

    Facilitator's Guide: *Crossroads*, Turning Point, P. O. Box 22127, Chattanooga, TN 37422-2127

However, if a man does not want to marry his brother's wife, she shall go to the elders at the town gate and say, "My husband's brother refuses to carry on his brother's name in Israel. He will not fulfill the duty of a brother-in-law to me." Then the elders of his town shall summon him and talk to him. If he persists in saying, "I do not want to marry her," his brother's widow shall go up to him in the presence of the elders, take off one of his sandals, spit in his face and say, "This is what is done to the man who will not build up his brother's family line." That man's line shall be known in Israel as The Family of the Unsandaled. (NIV)

Genesis 38:6-11

Judah got a wife for Er, his firstborn, and her name was Tamar. But Er, Judah's firstborn, was wicked in the Lord's sight; so the Lord put him to death.

Then Judah said to Onan, "Lie with your brother's wife and fulfill your duty to her as a brother-in-law to produce offspring for your brother." But Onan knew that the offspring would not be his; so whenever he lay with his brother's wife, he spilled his semen on the ground to keep from producing offspring for his brother. What he did was wicked in the Lord's sight; so he put him to death also.

Judah then said to his daughter-in-law Tamar, "Live as a widow in your father's house until my son Shelah grows up." For he thought, "He may die too, just like his brothers." So Tamar went to live in her father's house. (NIV)

What was Onan's sin?

Does this have anything to do with masturbation?

In the Old Testament, there were many things that made a person ceremonially unclean. Things that were clean were symbolic of holiness and dedication to God. Things that were called unclean were potentially harmful to the health of those who touched them, and some of them, such as leprosy, were symbolic of the results of human sin.

Leviticus 15:16-18

When a man has an emission of semen, he must bathe his whole body with water, and he will be unclean till evening. Any clothing or leather that has semen on it must be washed with water, and it will be unclean till evening. When a man lies with a woman and there is an emission of semen, both must bathe with water, and they will be unclean till evening. (NIV)

Now have the group read Genesis 38:6-11.

Onan refused to obey God and his father by honoring what later became the "Kinsman Redeemer" laws regarding Levite marriage. He was required by God's Law to produce a child for his dead brother.

No. It is actually the act of coitus interruptus, a form of birth control.

Deuteronomy 23:10-11

> If one of your men is unclean because of a nocturnal emission, he is to go outside the camp and stay there. But as evening approaches he is to wash himself, and at sunset he may return to the camp. (NIV)

Leviticus 15:19

> When a woman has her regular flow of blood, the impurity of her monthly period will last seven days, and anyone who touches her will be unclean till evening. (NIV)

What was the consequence of coming into contact with human semen?

> Being ceremonially unclean for a day.

Were things that caused one to be unclean always related to willful actions?

> Did a woman will her menstrual cycle? Did a leper decide to be leprous? What if a dead body fell on you? Did men choose to have "wet dreams"? Note also: A couple having sexual intercourse within the godly bonds of marriage still became unclean.

After masturbating, would a man be considered ceremonially unclean?

> Yes.

Since a woman can masturbate without an ejaculation, would she be considered ceremonially unclean?

> She was not made ceremonially unclean by it; hence, these laws did not apply to half the population.

What implications does this have to this discussion?

> It seems weak to base an argument on something that does not apply to all people.

Matthew 5:27-28

> You have heard that it was said, 'Do not commit adultery.' But I tell you that anyone who looks at a woman lustfully has already committed adultery with her in his heart. (NIV)

How does Jesus focus the overall issue in Matthew 5:27-28?

> It all boils down to lust.

  Facilitator's Guide: *Crossroads*, Turning Point, P. O. Box 22127, Chattanooga, TN 37422-2127

The Bible teaches that lust is sinful, destructive, and that we should run from it. Pornography is designed to stir lust in those who use it by helping them enter into a fantasy world where orgasm is the goal. For most people, exposure to pornographic material initially involves and continues to involve masturbation.

Is it possible to masturbate without lust?

List some possibilities if you think it is.

Personal response.

A preteen who discovers a pleasurable feeling is not "sexualizing" anyone. (Obviously there may come a time when the connection between the act and sexual thoughts are realized, and then it would become sinful.)

[Note—This question may raise the whole issue of how we define masturbation. It may be that lust is critical to the very definition.]

pplication

Allow 20 Minutes

In the final analysis, it is critical to separate the act from the motives of the heart. We must be careful not to use the number of times we masturbate per month as a gauge as to how good or bad we are. We must be careful not to use the number of times we masturbate per month as a legal standard as to how we are growing in Christ.

Should we make rules (laws) about something when the Bible does not specifically state such rules? (See Colossians 2:23.)

Rules may appear wise, but God says they are man-made religion and that rules cannot keep our flesh in line. Rules are not able...only grace is.

Many people act like if they reduce the number of times they masturbate per month, then they are doing well—that they are now somehow a better person. The fact may be that they are progressing and this is a good sign, but the fact also might be that while they are masturbating less, they are still "lusting their brains out." It is possible to bring outward behavior into control while the inner thoughts remain wicked.

Ask yourself why it is so important to determine whether or not masturbation is a sin. If you are seeking an excuse to continue your behavior, then you have to question your heart regarding the motives behind your biblical search. If you are seeking a clear condemnation in the hope that it will strengthen you in the struggle, then ask yourself: "If the Bible did clearly condemn it, would I really stop?" The Law has no power to stop us from sinning (Romans 7; 1 Corinthians 15:56; Colossians 2:23).

What does this tension of having to decide on an "individual" (case-by-case) basis ideally force us to do?

Go to God in the midst of it and seek his wisdom and grace. Instead of hiding behind easy rules, we are forced to actually talk to God about the particulars. We end up entering into relationship with Him.

Our desire needs to be that we serve God in all things—deeds and words and thoughts. Since the Bible is not clear on masturbation—though it is very clear on lust—we have to live with the tension of determining what is sin and what is not. We have to trust God for the moment. This makes us learn to rely on God instead of ourselves. Maybe this is why God does not give us a crystal-clear statement on masturbation, but he does give us crystal-clear guidance on avoiding lust and being mastered by anything other than his will.

"All things are lawful for me, but not all things are profitable. All things are lawful for me, but I will not be mastered by anything" (1 Corinthians 6:12, NASB).

What is the deeper issue in this question about masturbation?

The state of our heart and our attitudes towards God. Can God meet our needs? Are we willing to trust Him for the grace to obey, or are we going to do our own thing by taking control?

One Final Thought: Since masturbation focuses on giving oneself pleasure, separate from sacrificial relationship with the spouse, it appears to be a selfish act. It is a reflection of a selfish heart, and selfishness is the opposite of love.

Would you consider your orientation more selfish or more sacrificial?

Personal responses.

Closing Prayer

Pray for any specific needs group members may express. Pray for encouragement and wisdom for the group and that God will continually reveal our motives to us.

Session 3 The Lies of Pornography

Introduction

Allow 10 Minutes

Opening Prayer	Ask God for the ability to distinguish between truth and the lies of pornography.
Sharing Questions Share with the group a time when you were told a lie and accepted it for a fact. What were the consequences?	Personal response.

Self-Awareness

Allow 20-25 Minutes

NOTE TO FACILITATOR:

This lesson is fairly straightforward. A key point to stress is the intent of the pornographers to trap and enslave not only the people who work for them but also the people who use their product. The individuals in the group should not be allowed to wallow in a "victim mentality," but the reality of the fact that porn is designed to enslave is important to get across. In contrast to the lies of porn is the truth of the gospel. Emphasize the fact that there is a relational aspect of knowing the truth. We are called to be in relationship with Jesus, not just gain head knowledge.

Pornography is a huge moneymaking operation with revenues far exceeding the largest American corporations. It generated $56 billion worldwide in 1998 and is becoming a significant source of revenue for many people. Some young women, for example, are now paying their way through college simply by allowing themselves to be a Pay Per View offering on the Internet. It is obvious that one of the main motives of the industry is to attract men and get them to spend their money.

Since the goal is to get men to spend their money and keep coming back for more, we need to realize that the *product* is designed to be addictive. While women are less likely to be lured by pictorial porn, they can be seduced by chat rooms or romance novels. The lies and dynamics are very similar.

How has viewing pornography contributed to the addictive process in your life?

One of the reasons pornography is so enslaving is that it is built on a massive web of lies yet does not satisfy. The lies lure the customers in, and the lack of ultimate satisfaction leads them ever deeper into the web. The lies create a way of thinking in the customers that encourages them to seek more and spend more. The normal person engaged in viewing pornography continues to seek new images on a regular basis.

What are some common lies of the pornographic industry?

How do these lies affect the way you think about sex and your own sexuality?

Pornographers encourage people to engage in sexual sin so as to make a personal profit. Pornographers care nothing about the consequences of broken lives, just as long as they can make their profits. Seeing their lies and motives helps us see the truth about what is going on. Our desire for pornography is being fabricated and pushed upon us; and even though we do respond by our own lusts, it is important to see the way we are being manipulated and lied to.

Personal responses.

- Viewing pornography is a victimless crime.
- Women are insatiable sex maniacs.
- Women actually enjoy being raped.
- Incest is a good way of teaching your daughter about sexuality.
- Beauty is the most important thing in life.
- Bigger is better.
- Women are objects for men to enjoy.
- Deviations are normal and common.
- Frequent sex is necessary for good health.
- Masturbation is a desirable thing.
- Sex and intimacy are the same.

These lies warp our thinking about other people, making them into sexual objects for our pleasure. They also create desires in us for unique and immoral acts.

Facilitator's Guide: *Crossroads*, Turning Point, P. O. Box 22127, Chattanooga, TN 37422-2127

Spiritual Awareness Lead-In

"Surely in vain the net is spread in the sight of any bird" (Proverbs 1:17 KJV).

The Bible says it is useless to lay a net in front of a bird if it is looking, so our knowledge of the lies can help us reject them for the truth of God's Word.

How often do you think about the fact that the pornography industry is intentionally lying to you to lure you in? How does this make you feel about the pornography industry?

Answers will vary.

In your opinion, how does pornography impact "The Sin System" model?

It creates lust which impacts our beliefs about what kind of person we are, and it triggers preoccupation with sex.

Spiritual-Awareness

Allow 20-25 Minutes

Deuteronomy 7:1-6

When the LORD your God brings you into the land you are entering to possess and drives out before you many nations–the Hittites, Girgashites, Amorites, Canaanites, Perizzites, Hivites and Jebusites, seven nations larger and stronger than you—and when the LORD your God has delivered them over to you and you have defeated them, then you must destroy them totally. Make no treaty with them, and show them no mercy. Do not intermarry with them. Do not give your daughters to their sons or take their daughters for your sons, for they will turn your sons away from following me to serve other gods, and the LORD's anger will burn against you and will quickly destroy you. This is what you are to do to them: Break down their altars, smash their sacred stones, cut down their Asherah poles and burn their idols in the fire. For you are a people holy to the LORD your God. The LORD your God has chosen you out of all the peoples on the face of the earth to be his people, his treasured possession. (NIV)

Do these instructions seem reasonable to you?

Personal response.

What reasons can you think of that might explain such drastic actions?

In the Old Testament time period, there was a fertility cult in the Middle East that seduced the Israelites. God told them to totally destroy the pagan inhabitants of the land so they would not be tempted to follow their evil ways.

The Israelites did not obey and, as a result, left themselves open to severe temptations and moral corruption.

Because the drive for sex is so powerful, unscrupulous people have been making a profit from appealing to sinful sexual desire since ancient times.

Baal was a god of the Canaanite people who was worshiped by engaging in sex at his temples. The priests of Baal profited by providing prostitutes for the worshippers. The Israelites would engage in sex at the temple of Baal and then go to their own priests and give an offering seeking forgiveness for their sins. Because the Israelite priests were allowed to keep part of these offerings, they were motivated by greed to encourage people to commit even more sinful worship of Baal with prostitutes.

Hosea 4:7-10

> The more priests there are, the more they sin against me. They have exchanged the glory of God for the disgrace of idols. "The priests get fed when the people sin and bring their sin offerings to them. So the priests are glad when the people sin! 'Like priests, like people'—since the priests are wicked, the people are wicked, too. So now I will punish both priests and people for all their wicked deeds. They will eat and still be hungry. Though they do a big business as prostitutes, they will have no children, for they have deserted the Lord to worship other gods." (NLT)

The lust for money and the lust for sex combine to motivate countless people to believe that fulfillment can come from pursuing and acquiring both, but the *law of diminishing returns* prevents people from finding contentment.

How is the *law of diminishing returns* illustrated by these verses?

The *law of diminishing returns* is the idea that what satisfies today does not satisfy tomorrow. There is an insatiable appetite for more that is never satisfied. This is why there is the inevitable progression from *Playboy* to *Penthouse* to *Hustler* to hard-core pornography and deviant behaviors. The pornographers are **banking** on this inevitable sequence.

Describe how you think this principle works by giving other examples.

Personal responses.

Life experience shows us that the promises of fulfillment pornography offers are lies, but addictions blind us to the truth—making it easier for us to believe the lies the pornography industry is built upon.

John 8:43-45

> Why is my language not clear to you? Because you are unable to hear what I say. You belong to your father, the devil, and you want to carry out your father's desire. He was a murderer from the beginning, not holding to the truth, for there is no truth in him. When he lies, he speaks his native language, for he is a liar and the father of lies. Yet because I tell the truth, you do not believe me! (NIV)

In this passage, Jesus is addressing people who refuse to love him and seek to kill him.

According to Jesus: Why could these people not understand him? What is the source of lies?

They were not born again, so their natural desires were to be like their father, the devil. They were unable to recognize the truth Jesus was speaking.

The source of lies is the devil, who is the father of lies because lying is consistent with his very nature.

In contrast, what does Jesus say about himself in John 14:6?

He is the truth.

Romans 1:28-32

> Furthermore, since they did not think it worthwhile to retain the knowledge of God, he gave them over to a depraved mind, to do what ought not to be done. They have become filled with every kind of wickedness, evil, greed and depravity. They are full of envy, murder, strife, deceit and malice. They are gossips, slanderers, God-haters, insolent, arrogant and boastful; they invent ways of doing evil; they disobey their parents; they are senseless, faithless, heartless, ruthless. Although they know God's righteous decree that those who do such things deserve death, they not only continue to do these very things but also approve of those who practice them. (NIV)

What dangers result from rejecting God and the truth?

Rejecting God results in a degradation of our minds, as we are open to the deception of the devil. This can lead to a downward moral spiral that ends in enslavement to sin.

Proverbs 7:10-27

> The woman approached him, dressed seductively and sly of heart. She was the brash, rebellious type who never stays at home. She is often seen in the streets and markets, soliciting at every corner. She threw her arms around him and kissed him, and with a brazen look she said, "I've offered my sacrifices and just finished my vows. It's you I was looking for! I came out to find you, and here you are! My bed is spread with colored sheets of finest linen imported from Egypt. I've perfumed my bed with myrrh, aloes, and cinnamon. Come, let's drink our fill of love until morning. Let's enjoy each other's caresses, for my husband is not home. He's away on a long trip. He has taken a wallet full of money with him, and he won't return until later in the month." So she seduced him with her pretty speech. With her flattery she enticed him. He followed her at once, like an ox going to the slaughter or like a trapped stag, awaiting the arrow that would pierce its heart. He was like a bird flying into a snare, little knowing it would cost him his life. Listen to me, my sons, and pay attention to my words. Don't let your hearts stray away toward her. Don't wander down her wayward path. For she has been the ruin of many; numerous men have been her victims. Her house is the road to the grave. Her bedroom is the den of death. (NLT)

How is the behavior of the woman in this passage similar to the attractive promise of pornography?	This woman was seductive, brazen, promised pleasure, enticed the man by promising beautiful things, created a seductive environment, made him feel special, and planned to trap the man while not warning him of any danger.
What was the result?	The result was his death.

John 8:31-32

> Jesus therefore was saying to those Jews who had believed Him, "If you abide in My word, then you are truly disciples of Mine; and you shall know the truth, and the truth shall make you free." (NASB)

What promise does Jesus give us in John 8:31-32?	If we abide in His Word (obey what He says), we will know the truth, and the truth will set us free.
What kinds of things do we need to do to discover the *truth*?	Read the Bible and pray, seek counsel from other Christians.

The word *light* is often used to describe truth, and *darkness* is used to describe lies.

God's Word is truth, and it will always be against and destroy darkness. In John 1:1-5, we see that:

> In the beginning the Word already existed. He was with God, and he was God. He was in the beginning with God. He created everything there is. Nothing exists that he didn't make. Life itself was in him, and this life gives light to everyone. The light shines through the darkness, and the darkness can never extinguish it. (NLT)

What exposes lies and lying?	The truth of the Word of God.
How can you tell if someone is lying to you?	Comparing what we hear to the Word of God.
What do roaches do when you flip on the light? How does the light help you determine if you have roaches or crickets in your kitchen?	They are revealed and they flee. By seeing the insect in the light, you can determine what it is. The light makes the difference.

Facilitator's Guide: *Crossroads*, Turning Point, P. O. Box 22127, Chattanooga, TN 37422-2127

The lies of pornography are subtle and entice many people to a live a degraded lifestyle. To combat lies, everything must be compared to the truth of God's Word.

There are two critical aspects to truth in the Bible. First, truth is objective. It is given to us as Jesus Christ himself and as the written Word of the Bible. This objective aspect of truth is vital for our restoration because we can each go to it and have a standard. The written truth and Jesus as the truth prevent relativism and personal preferences. Evil is evil and good is good. Objective truth appeals to the mind and gives us a worldview by which to live. The Bible tells us, in fact, that transformation comes by having our minds renewed (Romans 12:2). If there is no such thing as objective truth, then there is no such thing as ethics and morals—each person can do whatever he or she wants. Chaos is the result.

Second, since the truth is Jesus, there is a relational aspect to it. It is by knowing Jesus personally that we can be assured that the truth is working in our lives and setting us free from our sin. Objective truth alone is not living and vital—a carved stone may have a truth on it, but a stone will not seek you out and pursue you in your sins. Jesus is the truth, and Jesus seeks relationship with us. We can know that Jesus is active in our lives, shining His light into our dark corners and revealing the lies we have believed as truth. Jesus will actively work in our hearts to change us and free us from the snares laid by wicked pornographers.

To resist the lies of the enemy, we must live in and with the truth. It must be part of who we are and occupy our minds constantly.

Look back at the question about the lies of pornography in the Self-Awareness section of this lesson.

What biblical truths would you use to confront each of these lies?

> Personal response.

What practical steps can you begin to take right now to live in the truth?

> Bible memorization, study, discussion with others, praying without ceasing, walking in the Spirit, accountable relationships, Bible teaching, resisting the devil, avoiding tempting situations.

Which of these steps will you take this week?

> Personal response.

Closing Prayer

> Pray for any specific needs group members may express. Pray for encouragement and wisdom for the group and for the spiritual discernment to recognize the lies we are told.

Introduction

Allow 10 Minutes

Opening Prayer	Ask God for the ability to understand the influence our upbringing has had on our behaviors and for the wisdom to know what to do with this knowledge.
Sharing Questions What is the earliest lesson you can remember learning from your parents or caregivers when you were growing up?	Personal response.

Self-Awareness

Allow 20-25 Minutes

NOTE TO FACILITATOR:

This lesson can be quite intense if the members begin to seriously share about their relationships with their parents and/or the things that happened to them as children. Be prepared for the possibility of someone's getting quite emotional.

The human family is supposed to provide nurture and support for the upbringing of children. God created the family for the purpose of passing on the gospel (Psalm 78:5-8) and for nurture. The family helps form the personality and values of a person. This can have very positive results when things are done biblically, but it can also have very negative results when the family is *messed up* and sin enters in.

When it comes to sexual sins, it is not uncommon to discover sin patterns going down through families—generation after generation. How many men who struggle with pornography had fathers who looked at pornography? How many men who struggle with homosexuality had a childhood homosexual encounter with a relative? It is a known fact that most child abusers were abused as children.

This dynamic of one generation's choices impacting future generations is described in the following passage:

> You shall not make for yourself an idol, or any likeness of what is in heaven above or on the earth beneath or in the water under the earth. You shall not worship them or serve them; for I, the LORD your God, am a jealous God, visiting the iniquity of the fathers on the children, on the third and the fourth generations of those who hate Me, but showing loving kindness to thousands, to those who love Me and keep My commandments (Exodus 20:4-6 NASB).

What does this passage tell us about the impact of a parent's sin on the generations that follow?

The second commandment states that God will visit the iniquity of the fathers upon the children, grandchildren, and even great-grandchildren.

Read the following passage:

> Yet you say, "Why should the son not bear the punishment for the father's iniquity?" When the son has practiced justice and righteousness, and has observed all My statutes and done them, he shall surely live. The person who sins will die. The son will not bear the punishment for the father's iniquity, nor will the father bear the punishment for the son's iniquity; the righteousness of the righteous will be upon himself, and the wickedness of the wicked will be upon himself (Ezekiel 18:19-20 NASB).

How does this passage clarify the meaning of Exodus 20:4-6?

In Ezekiel 18:19-20, God specifically tells us that each individual person bears the punishment for his or her own sin. No one is punished for another person's sin, even a parent's sin. The term "visit" is different from the idea of punishment. God does not punish children for their parents' sins, but the sins of the parents do visit the children. This means that there are consequences of sins that may impact the following generations.

There is no escaping the influence that our family of origin has in our lives. We are all influenced by the behaviors and attitudes we acquired from our interaction with our families. Many influences were positive, but even in the best of families, some were negative. It is important for us to understand the influence the past has on our present thinking and behaviors.

At the same time, it is important to understand that the purpose for reflecting on our family systems is not to shift blame or avoid our own personal responsibilities. If we engage in blame-shifting, we make matters worse for ourselves. Adam tried this tactic after he sinned in the Garden of Eden. King David tried to justify his sin with Bathsheba but was tormented by it. Only *after* David confessed was he able to find healing.

In the same way, we must take personal responsibility for how we have responded to our situations and for the sinful choices we have made. This lesson focuses on family background in an effort to understand the roots of our choices and so that we can start making new choices, not so that we can blame others.

Spiritual Awareness Lead–In

What positive influences were passed on to you from your family?

Personal responses.

What negative influences can you identify?

Personal responses.

Spiritual-Awareness

Allow 20-25 Minutes

In the times the Old Testament was written, it was common for families to pass small statues of their gods on to the next generation. This was a problem even among the Hebrews who knew God's commandment prohibiting idolatry. An example of someone possessing such an idol can be found in 1 Samuel 19:11-17.

Families today may not have statues of gods they pass from generation to generation, but they do pass along idols of sinful influences, behaviors, and attitudes to succeeding generations.

We may not have golden statues in our homes, but what kinds of family idols do we have?

Examples of these are materialism; drug and alcohol addictions; racism; sexual attitudes regarding women and pornography; overvaluing sports; spiritual, emotional or physical neglect or abuse, among many others.

The Bible is rich with examples of people who passed along their sins to their offspring. Isaac imitated his father Abraham's example.

Read the following passages:

Genesis 20:1-11

Now Abraham moved on from there into the region of the Negev and lived between Kadesh and Shur. For a while he stayed in Gerar, and there Abraham said of his wife Sarah, "She is my sister." Then Abimelech king of Gerar sent for Sarah and took her.

But God came to Abimelech in a dream one night and said to him, "You are as good as dead because of the woman you have taken; she is a married woman."

Now Abimelech had not gone near her, so he said, "Lord, will you destroy an innocent nation? Did he not say to me, 'She is my sister,' and didn't she also say, 'He is my brother'? I have done this with a clear conscience and clean hands."

Then God said to him in the dream, "Yes, I know you did this with a clear conscience, and so I have kept you from sinning against me. That is why I did not let you touch her. Now return the man's wife, for he is a prophet, and he will pray for you and you will live. But if you do not return her, you may be sure that you and all yours will die."

Early the next morning Abimelech summoned all his officials, and when he told them all that had happened, they were very much afraid. Then Abimelech called Abraham in and said, "What have you done to us? How have I wronged you that you have brought such great guilt upon me and my kingdom? You have done things to me that should not be done." And Abimelech asked Abraham, "What was your reason for doing this?"

Abraham replied, "I said to myself, 'There is surely no fear of God in this place, and they will kill me because of my wife.' (NIV)

Genesis 26:6-11

So Isaac stayed in Gerar.

When the men of that place asked him about his wife, he said, "She is my sister," because he was afraid to say, "She is my wife." He thought, "The men of this place might kill me on account of Rebekah, because she is beautiful."

When Isaac had been there a long time, Abimelech king of the Philistines looked down from a window and saw Isaac caressing his wife Rebekah. So Abimelech summoned Isaac and said, "She is really your wife! Why did you say, 'She is my sister'?"

Isaac answered him, "Because I thought I might lose my life on account of her."

Then Abimelech said, "What is this you have done to us? One of the men might well have slept with your wife, and you would have brought guilt upon us."

So Abimelech gave orders to all the people: "Anyone who molests this man or his wife shall surely be put to death." (NIV)

What behavior did Isaac imitate from his father Abraham?

Isaac followed the example of Abraham in lying to protect himself from harm.

David's sons, Amnon, Absolom, and Solomon, are mentioned in the following chapters.

2 Samuel 11:1-4

In the spring, at the time when kings go off to war, David sent Joab out with the king's men and the whole Israelite army. They destroyed the Ammonites and besieged Rabbah. But David remained in Jerusalem.

One evening David got up from his bed and walked around on the roof of the palace. From the roof he saw a woman bathing. The woman was very beautiful, and David sent someone to find out about her. The man said, "Isn't this Bathsheba, the daughter of Eliam and the wife of Uriah the Hittite?" Then David sent messengers to get her. She came to him, and he slept with her. (She had purified herself from her uncleanness.) Then she went back home. (NIV)

2 Samuel 13:1-15

In the course of time, Amnon son of David fell in love with Tamar, the beautiful sister of Absalom son of David.

Amnon became frustrated to the point of illness on account of his sister Tamar, for she was a virgin, and it seemed impossible for him to do anything to her.

Facilitator's Guide: *Crossroads*, Turning Point, P. O. Box 22127, Chattanooga, TN 37422-2127

Now Amnon had a friend named Jonadab son of Shimeah, David's brother. Jonadab was a very shrewd man. He asked Amnon, "Why do you, the king's son, look so haggard morning after morning? Won't you tell me?"

Amnon said to him, "I'm in love with Tamar, my brother Absalom's sister."

"Go to bed and pretend to be ill," Jonadab said. "When your father comes to see you, say to him, 'I would like my sister Tamar to come and give me something to eat. Let her prepare the food in my sight so I may watch her and then eat it from her hand.' "

So Amnon lay down and pretended to be ill. When the king came to see him, Amnon said to him, "I would like my sister Tamar to come and make some special bread in my sight, so I may eat from her hand."

David sent word to Tamar at the palace: "Go to the house of your brother Amnon and prepare some food for him." So Tamar went to the house of her brother Amnon, who was lying down. She took some dough, kneaded it, made the bread in his sight and baked it. Then she took the pan and served him the bread, but he refused to eat.

"Send everyone out of here," Amnon said. So everyone left him. Then Amnon said to Tamar, "Bring the food here into my bedroom so I may eat from your hand." And Tamar took the bread she had prepared and brought it to her brother Amnon in his bedroom. But when she took it to him to eat, he grabbed her and said, "Come to bed with me, my sister."

"Don't, my brother!" she said to him. "Don't force me. Such a thing should not be done in Israel! Don't do this wicked thing. What about me? Where could I get rid of my disgrace? And what about you? You would be like one of the wicked fools in Israel. Please speak to the king; he will not keep me from being married to you." But he refused to listen to her, and since he was stronger than she, he raped her.

Then Amnon hated her with intense hatred. In fact, he hated her more than he had loved her. Amnon said to her, "Get up and get out!" (NIV)

2 Samuel 16:20-23

Absalom said to Ahithophel, "Give us your advice. What should we do?"

Ahithophel answered, "Lie with your father's concubines whom he left to take care of the palace. Then all Israel will hear that you have made yourself a stench in your father's nostrils, and the hands of everyone with you will be strengthened." So they pitched a tent for Absalom on the roof, and he lay with his father's concubines in the sight of all Israel.

Now in those days the advice Ahithophel gave was like that of one who inquires of God. That was how both David and Absalom regarded all of Ahithophel's advice. (NIV)

1 Kings 11:3-8

He had seven hundred wives of royal birth and three hundred concubines, and his wives led him astray. As Solomon grew old, his wives turned his heart after other gods, and his heart was not fully devoted to the LORD his God, as the heart of David his father had been. He followed Ashtoreth the goddess of the Sidonians, and Molech the detestable god of the Ammonites. So Solomon did evil in the eyes of the LORD; he did not follow the LORD completely, as David his father had done.

On a hill east of Jerusalem, Solomon built a high place for Chemosh the detestable god of Moab, and for Molech the detestable god of the Ammonites. He did the same for all his foreign wives, who burned incense and offered sacrifices to their gods. (NIV)

What example did these sons of David follow?

These sons of David followed him in committing sexual sin.

There are several common family factors that influence the development of sinful sexual behaviors. The four most important are:

Childhood Abuse—Sexual, physical, or verbal abuse all impact a child's concept of self and his or her understanding of what it means to be a sexual being. Neglect is also a form of abuse in that the child is given the message that he or she is not important and must find ways of looking after him or herself. The victim of abuse may become a victimizer as he or she lives out the lessons of childhood.

Real or Perceived Abandonment—Divorce, death, long-term work-related travel, or even chronic illness of one of the parents can impact a child. The lack of relationship or the fact of no relationship may create a desire to pursue relationships even in sinful ways. The child may grow to fear relationships or to have relationships that he or she believes can be controlled.

Attitudes Towards Sex—There are two extremes in how a household may treat the subject of sexuality: promiscuously or severely inhibited. Growing up in a promiscuous household may teach a child that intimacy is based on being sexual. Growing up in a home where sex was never discussed may cre-

Facilitator's Guide: *Crossroads*, Turning Point, P. O. Box 22127, Chattanooga, TN 37422-2127

ate a sense that sex is dirty or evil. A child may be ignorant and find his or her information on the subject through sources of misinformation like pornography and other children.

Role Models—Parents are to model what it means to be male and female, and this is ideally done when both parents are lovingly accessible to the child. When one or both parents present distorted images of masculinity and femininity, a child may develop distorted and sinful ways of relating to individuals of the same and opposite sex.

Which, if any, of these factors have influenced your behaviors as an adult.

Personal response.

What was your parents' attitude towards sexuality? Did they discuss it? Did you ever see them show physical affection to each other?

Answers will vary. Focus on how attitudes and events have shaped the person's present thinking.

How did this shape your own thinking?

Answers will vary.

What sins of the fathers do you see in your own family? Did you discover a stash of pornography at home?

Answers will vary. Realize that this sharing may be very emotional and intense. Be sensitive to the needs of the individual but also be careful that too much graphic detail is not shared because you do not want the sharing to become a stumbling block for others. People should be able to describe events without describing details.

What kind of relationship did you have with your parents?

Personal response.

How did this encourage or discourage the sinful responses you have learned?

Personal response.

How do you see yourself repeating patterns?

Personal response.

What promises do the following verses give?

1 John 1:9

> If we confess our sins, he is faithful and just and will forgive us our sins and purify us from all unrighteousness. (NIV)

Romans 12:1-2

> Therefore, I urge you, brothers, in view of God's mercy, to offer your bodies as living sacrifices, holy and pleasing to God—this is your spiritual act of worship. Do not conform any longer to the

pattern of this world, but be transformed by the renewing of your mind. Then you will be able to test and approve what God's will is—his good, pleasing and perfect will. (NIV)

2 Corinthians 1:3-5

Praise be to the God and Father of our Lord Jesus Christ, the Father of compassion and the God of all comfort, who comforts us in all our troubles, so that we can comfort those in any trouble with the comfort we ourselves have received from God. For just as the sufferings of Christ flow over into our lives, so also through Christ our comfort overflows. (NIV)

pplication

Allow 20 Minutes

Though our actions are our free choices, it often seems like we have been acting certain ways for so long that we no longer really have a choice. Often we feel *programmed* to behave the way we do. The truth is that we may have learned our behavior years ago and at such an early age that we **do** seem to have little control now. The concept of the *sins of the fathers* helps teach us the origins of our behavior. Our choices are still **our** choices, but knowing what may be fueling the choice helps us to stop making that choice.

Often there is a need for the healing of relationships within the family. (This is the subject of another lesson.) Right now, do not pass the blame but understand that your parents also were part of a chain of *sins of the fathers* coming down to them. The hope that we have is that God can stop this continual passing down of sinful behaviors. God promises to bless thousands of those who love Him (Exodus 20:6).

God also offers forgiveness to us as well as taking our burdens from us. He offers to renew our minds and hence change our behaviors. He offers us a community in which to be strengthened by accountability and encouragement. Be renewed knowing that God can and will stop the passing on of these sinful behaviors. You are in the generation that can stop it. Decide that you want to be the end of the line!

A life of sinful disobedience is the pathway to an empty life. In the following passage, the forefathers are said to have handed down an empty way of life. If you have been handed down a life inclined toward sexual addiction, you need help to overcome. This help is found in Christ.

For you know that it was not with perishable things such as silver or gold that you were redeemed from the empty way of life handed down to you from your forefathers, but with the precious blood of Christ, a lamb without blemish or defect. He was chosen before the creation of the world, but was revealed in these last times for your sake. Through him you believe in God, who raised him from the dead and glorified him, and so your faith and hope are in God.

Now that you have purified yourselves by obeying the truth so that you have sincere love for your brothers, love one another deeply, from the heart. For you have been born again, not of perishable seed, but of imperishable, through the living and enduring word of God (1 Peter 1:18-23 NIV).

What are some ideas outlined in this passage that can help us overcome the family influences that encourage sexual sin?

- Recognize that Christ has died to "redeem" us, that is, to pay for our release from the empty way of life we are trapped in.
- Recognize that God has loved us so much that he has paid the highest price possible to give us this new life.
- Recognize that God planned this from before the world was created.
- Recognize that we purify ourselves by obeying the truth and trusting in God. This helps us develop new patterns of living.
- Recognize that we have a more significant family than the family that raised us. We are born again, and this birth initiated us into a family with a perfect Father. In this family, we will never be abandoned or influenced toward sin because our Father is a Holy God.

Closing Prayer

Pray for enduring hope in the faithfulness of God. Pray for specific needs expressed by the group.

Session 5 *False Intimacy*

Introduction

Allow 10 Minutes

Opening Prayer

> Give thanks to God that he is always near and that he loves us unconditionally.

Sharing Questions

If you were stranded alone on an island, who would you miss most? Why?

> Personal response.

Would God's presence with you be an adequate comfort?

> Personal response.

Self-Awareness

Allow 20-25 Minutes

> NOTE TO FACILITATOR:
>
> Some group members may not understand that sexual addictions involve more than the simple desire for more sex. The need for intimacy also fuels many addictions. Of course, we are all responsible for our choices when we follow after our lusts, and these choices can lead to the circle of guilt and shame known as the "sin system." In this cycle, we feel increasingly alienated from God, those we love, and ourselves. To fill the emptiness left by this break, many people try to find comfort by acting out sexually, hoping to find meaningful relationships—only to experience what has been called false intimacy.

"If sex is the issue, then why can I have great sex with my wife and an hour later, while in the grocery store getting munchies, find myself looking lustfully at a beautiful woman? You would think I would be satisfied with what I just had!"

This comment is not as uncommon as you might imagine. Many men can have frequent, satisfying sex with their wives and yet still be on the prowl within hours. What is it they are seeking? What is missing? Why is it a man can masturbate numerous times in one day and still feel the need for more—even beyond his physical capacity?

Dr. Harry W. Schaumburg in his book, *False Intimacy*, makes a clear case for the idea that what is really being sought in illicit

Facilitator's Guide: *Crossroads*, Turning Point, P. O. Box 22127, Chattanooga, TN 37422-2127

relationships or through pornography is intimacy. What men (and women) are seeking is an intimate relationship. The problem is that sexual intercourse alone is not true intimacy unless there is a deep and flowing relationship combined with it. This is why sex without relationship is ultimately unfulfilling. Since sex alone cannot meet this need and leaves the man (or woman) feeling empty inside, there is the pursuit of another encounter or relationship. The false intimacy does not satisfy and leads to more false intimacy. A cycle is created and bondage ensues.

To add to the problem, the porn industry works to create an image of intimacy; but because pornography breaks intimate relationships, fantasized intimacy is created and reinforced. The phone sex lines, Internet chat rooms, lap dances and escort services all conspire to give the impression that the woman (or man) cares about the customer. What happens, however, if the customer is unable to pay for the service? There may be an occasional *free* teaser service, but what if the customer is not able to pay for more? How much love and concern is there for the customer then? The illusion of intimacy is developed by the industry to make money.

What are some ways that pornography offers an illusion of intimacy?

It appeals to our core sexuality and offers us a relationship without the problems of actually relating to a person. A fantasy relationship is controlled and cannot surprise us. A fantasy relationship does not force us to give up our own wants and desires.

How might chat-rooms, phone sex, and even escorts also give the illusion of intimacy?

Again, the women (or men) know what to say and how to act interested and caring. They may give the respect that is so hungered for. They will act out fantasies. In chat rooms people can hide behind false names and pretend to be someone they really are unable to be in reality. In chat rooms, relationships can be ended with a click, so there is no real commitment.

In the case of men and women who have affairs or pick up partners at bars or in other locations, the same dynamic is often in play. Though there may seem to be a deeper level of intimacy in the case of an affair, in the final analysis, it is following a pattern of false intimacy that the relationship only masks. The issues that precipitate an extramarital relationship are never solved by the extramarital relationship.

How could a one-night stand or even a prolonged affair give the illusion of intimacy?

One-night stands obviously are times of intense attraction and sexual release, but later they seem shallow. An ongoing affair may seem intimate—the individuals may actually have deeper conversations than with their spouses—but the relationship is built on lies and deceit. It is not a relationship built on self-sacrifice. If the person is willing to cheat on a spouse, this reveals a high level of selfishness. Affairs rarely last due to this selfish core. The intimacy is an illusion since the individuals are not truly interested in the well-being of the other as much as their own personal needs.

Spiritual Awareness Lead–In

Before his conversion to Christ, St. Augustine followed a lifestyle of sexual impurity. He later came to the conclusion that God made us for himself and our hearts find no peace till they rest in him.

How do you think this insight relates to the pursuit of false intimacy?

Augustine summarizes the truth of our personal realities—that we are made in God's image and will never have inner peace until we have peace with him. We are created for relationship with Him, and everything else leaves us feeling empty.

Spiritual-Awareness

Allow 20-25 Minutes

As Dr. Schaumburg states in *False Intimacy*, if what we seek to fill with sexual activity is the need for intimate relationship, then we must have been designed from the beginning for connectedness with God and others. Read the following verses:

Genesis 2:7

Then the LORD God formed man of dust from the ground, and breathed into his nostrils the breath of life; and man became a living being. (NASB)

What do you see in this verse that communicates God's intimate involvement with the first human being?

He carefully formed the first man from the dust of the ground and came close and breathed into his nostrils. Through this intimate contact with the Creator, man became a living being.

Genesis 2:18

Then the LORD God said, "It is not good for the man to be alone; I will make him a helper suitable for him." (NASB)

What do these well-known words of God teach us about the need for relationships?

Human relationship is critical to a person's well-being. We are created to be relational.

Genesis 2:19–25

And out of the ground the LORD God formed every beast of the field and every bird of the sky, and brought them to the man to see what he would call them; and whatever the man called a living creature, that was its name. And the man gave names to all the cattle, and to the birds of the sky, and to every beast of the field, but for Adam there was not found a helper suitable for him. So the LORD God caused a deep sleep to fall upon the man, and he slept; then He took one of his ribs, and closed up the flesh at that place. And the LORD God fashioned into a woman the rib which He had taken from the man, and brought her to the man. And the man said, "This is now bone of my bones, And flesh of my flesh; She shall be called Woman, Because she was taken out of Man." For this cause a man shall leave his father and his mother, and shall cleave to his wife; and they shall become one flesh. And the man and his wife were both naked and were not ashamed. (NASB)

What do you see in these verses that communicates man's intimate involvement with the first woman?

Woman was formed from deep within man; they were of the same body, formed with great care by God. They shared the same life that God had breathed into man. They were one flesh, and God's design for every union as "one flesh" was begun. They were together, totally exposed to one another with no thought of hiding anything from each other.

The Bible teaches us that this connectedness with God and others was broken by a human's choice to disobey God.

Genesis 3:2-8

And the woman said to the serpent, "From the fruit of the trees of the garden we may eat; but from the fruit of the tree which is in the middle of the garden, God has said, 'You shall not eat from it or touch it, lest you die.' " And the serpent said to the woman, "You surely shall not die! For God knows that in the day you eat from it your eyes will be opened, and you will be like God, knowing good and evil." When the woman saw that the tree was good for food, and that it was a delight to the eyes, and that the tree was desirable to make one wise, she took from its fruit and ate; and she gave also to her husband with her, and he ate. Then the eyes of both of them were opened, and they knew that they were naked; and they sewed fig leaves together and made themselves loin coverings. And they heard the sound of the LORD God walking in the garden in the cool of the day, and the man and his wife hid themselves from the presence of the LORD God among the trees of the garden. (NASB)

What did the man and woman do when their eyes were opened after eating the fruit?

> The man and woman covered their bodies, no longer confident to be totally exposed without shame. They hid themselves from God.

What do think this symbolizes?

> It symbolizes an end to perfect intimacy between themselves and God. Sin destroys intimacy.

Genesis 3:9-24

Then the LORD God called to the man, and said to him, "Where are you?" And he said, "I heard the sound of Thee in the garden, and I was afraid because I was naked; so I hid myself." And He said, "Who told you that you were naked? Have you eaten from the tree of which I commanded you not to eat?" And the man said, "The woman whom Thou gavest to be with me, she gave me from the tree, and I ate." Then the LORD God said to the woman, "What is this you have done?" And the woman said, "The serpent deceived me, and I ate." And the LORD God said to the serpent, "Because you have done this, Cursed are you more than all cattle, And more than every beast of the field; On your belly shall you go, And dust shall you eat All the days of your life; And I will put enmity Between you and the woman, And between your seed and her seed; He shall bruise you on the head, And you shall bruise him on the heel." To the woman He said, "I will greatly multiply Your pain in childbirth, In pain you shall bring forth children; Yet your desire shall be for your husband, And he shall rule over you." Then to Adam He said, "Because you have listened to the voice of your wife, and have eaten from the tree about which I commanded you, saying, 'You shall not eat from it'; Cursed is the ground because of you; In toil you shall eat of it All the days of your life. "Both thorns and thistles it shall grow for you; And you shall eat the plants of the field; By the sweat of your face You shall eat bread, Till you return to the ground, Because from it you were taken; For you are dust, And to dust you shall return." Now the man called his wife's name Eve, because she was the mother of all the living. And the LORD God made garments of skin for Adam and his wife, and clothed them. Then the LORD God said, "Behold, the man has become like one of Us, knowing good and evil; and now, lest he stretch out his hand, and take also from the tree of life, and eat, and live forever"—therefore the LORD God sent him out from the garden of Eden, to cultivate the ground from which he was taken. So He drove the man out; and at the east of the garden of Eden He stationed the cherubim, and the flaming sword which turned every direction, to guard the way to the tree of life. (NASB)

How did the disobedience of the first humans impact their intimate relationship with God and each other?

They hid from Him; competition was begun between them (v16b); the way God provided for them was forever changed (vv17-19); physical death became a reality (v19); and they were driven from God's intimate presence.

Romans 1:21-24

For although they knew God, they neither glorified him as God nor gave thanks to him, but their thinking became futile and their foolish hearts were darkened. Although they claimed to be wise, they became fools and exchanged the glory of the immortal God for images made to look like mortal man and birds and animals and reptiles.

Therefore God gave them over in the sinful desires of their hearts to sexual impurity for the degrading of their bodies with one another. (NIV)

Since humans were created for intimacy with each other and with God and this intimacy has been severely damaged, is it any wonder we seek to find intimacy in misdirected ways?

What does this passage teach about our reaction to God, even to this day?

Instead of seeking relationship with God, we seek to fill ourselves with what the world can offer, resulting in a bondage to sin and impurity.

What started out good in the Garden of Eden is now twisted under the effects of sin. Relationship with God is changed. Relationships with other people are changed. Sin has entered in, and what used to be good desires and needs—relationships with God and with other people—are now corrupted. By seeking the world to satisfy us, we get further and further from God.

If we are created for relationship with God and in our sin we are striving to fill this with worldly things, then we will never be satisfied. Worldly things can never meet our need for God. If they could, then God would be expendable. The only way to get into the core of the sinful behavior—and begin to have real success—is to start to deal with this core need for relationship with God. Our goal cannot be simply to *fix* ourselves or even to have a better relationship with our spouse. Our goal must be to have a deeper relationship with God. Only this will fill the void. Of course, this means we cannot do it alone. Relationships involve two individuals, and in this case, the other is God. Call out to God and ask Him to restore your relationship. He must be involved.

> But this is the new covenant I will make with the people of Israel on that day, says the Lord: I will put my laws in their minds so they will understand them, and I will write them on their hearts so they will obey them. I will be their God, and they will be my people.
>
> And they will not need to teach their neighbors, nor will they need to teach their family, saying, "You should know the Lord." For everyone, from the least to the greatest, will already know me.
>
> And I will forgive their wrongdoings, and I will never again remember their sins (Hebrews 8:10-12 NLT).

What promises do you see in this passage?

God will enable us to understand and obey his laws because they will become part of us; he will be our God, and we will be his people; we will all know God, every one of us; and he will forgive us and never remember our sins.

Do you think that a relationship with a spouse can be a case of false intimacy? Explain briefly.

The wife or husband can be seen merely as someone who can provide for the needs of the other. Sex can be little more than a physical act—often akin to rape. Individuals may feel they are close because they have great sex together; but beyond that act, they do not talk or enjoy each other's company.

1 Corinthians 13 is a familiar passage that can teach us a lot about a relationship of love that leads to true intimacy.

> Love is patient and kind. Love is not jealous or boastful or proud or rude. Love does not demand its own way. Love is not irritable, and it keeps no record of when it has been wronged. It is never glad about injustice but rejoices whenever the truth wins out. Love never gives up, never loses faith, is always hopeful, and endures through every circumstance (4-7 NLT).

How is the love described here different from the love expressed in the world of the sexually addicted?

Love in the sexually addicted world is based on what I can get to satisfy myself. The love described in 1 Corinthians 13 is unselfish, caring for another without being selfish, and comes from God through intimacy with him.

What advice do you have for someone who wants to grow in a more intimate relationship with God?

Answers will vary—spend time with God, pray, listen for his guidance, read the Bible, stop hiding, be honest, obey his commandments, etc. The real point, however, is to want to know him for who he is and not just for what we can get from him.

Closing Prayer

Pray for God to develop in the members a desire for him. Pray that the group members will love God because he is God, not because of what he does for them.

Session 6 *Spiritual Warfare*

Introduction

Allow 10 Minutes

Opening Prayer

Pray for strength to fight the "good fight" of faith.

Sharing Questions

Why do you think some people enjoy scary movies?

or

Why do you think evil intrigues some people?

Personal response.

Personal response.

Self-Awareness

Allow 20-25 Minutes

NOTE TO FACILITATOR:

There is something about our sinful human nature that likes to talk about the demonic and Satan, much like children like ghost stories. It is important that the group not focus excessively on Satan and his power. We are not to revere Satan, though we should respect him as a very dangerous enemy (1 Peter 5:8). Avoid getting into discussions that take the focus off of God and his grace and dwell on Satan and his power. Also realize that differing Christian denominations have different approaches to the subject of exorcism and spiritual warfare. Keep the talk on what the Bible says. Do not get into prolonged discussions of subjective events. Note also the difference between valid spiritual warfare and "quick fix" approaches that do not deal with the inner heart issues and the need for the renewing of the mind. Realize that it is possible to circumvent sanctifica-

Facilitator's Guide: *Crossroads*, Turning Point, P. O. Box 22127, Chattanooga, TN 37422-2127

It is so easy to get so focused on our predispositions toward sexual sin—to concentrate on our backgrounds and problems and propensity to sin—that we become totally "materialistic" in our approach. We think that if we can sort out our childhood, then we will have a handle on our behavior and change will occur. We think that if we can just get enough counseling and advice, things will—by necessity—improve. We think that if we can memorize enough Bible verses or concentrate on enough spiritual disciplines like prayer, devotions, and worship, the temptations will wane.

Ask the group members to discuss some of the strategies they have tried, believing that if they could just change something about themselves, understand themselves better, or do something, they would be free of their compulsive sexual sin. Were the strategies successful?

Personal response.

There is a missing component in this. We neglect the idea that we are up against an enemy who is intentional and has a specific plan of attack. We neglect the idea that, while we can do much to stop our own "contribution" to the problem, this is actually a war where we are up against a very real enemy. There is a definite satanic dimension to sexual sin. In one way, we might say that Satan has worked for years grooming us to be enslaved in the way we are. He may have laid the groundwork in our parents—the sins of the fathers—and then built on that during our young years. Patterns were created—with our sinful participation—that have deepened like ruts in a road through continual use. Events happened which were used by Satan to link into these predispositions and, like seed in fertile ground, have grown to produce bitter fruit. The chains have been forged a link at a time, both by predispositions, events, and our own willing sins.

As we attempt to walk free of those chains, we have to realize that the enemy is intentional in bringing temptations in our lives which will throw us off. The power of the temptations comes from the fact that they fit like a glove to our established sin patterns. Satan, through his minions, has set the triggers in our hearts and knows exactly how to fire them. It is no coincidence that a man with a weakness for women in short skirts will see a woman in a short skirt just after praying for greater holiness. It is no coincidence that the day *after* coming to an accountability meeting, a man will discover he has unrestricted access to the Internet and has been left alone for an hour.

Give some examples from your experience when it seemed to you that a "personalized" temptation came your way.

Personal response.

It is critical that we become alert to the dynamic that there are no "random" events. We have to be alert to the fact that we are being intentionally attacked and in ways that are fine-tuned to *our* own particular weakness. (Example: A man who struggles with homosexual desires is not going to be attacked by the temptation of a woman in a short skirt. Instead, while on his way to church, he will see a muscular man jogging with only sneakers and shorts on.) Name your particular weakness and know this is where you will be attacked. Sometimes the attacks hit weaknesses we did not even know we had. Like a "mole" in the world of political espionage, some of our weaknesses were planted years ago and suddenly surface without warning.

To what extent have you thought that the temptation you face in the area of your weakness is the result of a deliberate plan to undermine your spiritual growth?

Personal response.

Know who is behind all this and consciously fight him. Seek the grace and mercy of Christ in this battle—you cannot do it alone. Since our enemy is intentional and plotting, we really need the power of God found through prayer and his grace.

Spiritual Awareness Lead–In

Almost everyone has been in a physical fight at some time in his or her life. Think about the most violent physical conflict in which you were engaged.

How did you feel before the conflict began? What surprised you most during the conflict? How did you feel when the battle was over?

Most people are surprised by the ferocity of the conflict, especially when they are hit for the first time. Many Christians are not aware of the ferocity of the spiritual battles they face.

One of the enemies we face in our war with sin is the devil. The Bible teaches that he is in a rage against us and will be our enemy until the end comes.

Revelation 12:17

> So the dragon was enraged with the woman, and went off to make war with the rest of her children, who keep the commandments of God and hold to the testimony of Jesus. (NASB)

1 Peter 5:8-9

> Be of sober spirit, be on the alert. Your adversary, the devil, prowls about like a roaring lion, seeking someone to devour.
>
> But resist him, firm in your faith, knowing that the same experiences of suffering are being accomplished by your brethren who are in the world. (NASB)

What strategies for dealing with the devil's assaults do you see in these verses?

> Have a sober spirit; be alert; resist him, firm in faith; take comfort that others are facing the same thing.

Proverbs 7:21-27

> With persuasive words she led him astray; she seduced him with her smooth talk. All at once he followed her like an ox going to the slaughter, like a deer stepping into a noose till an arrow pierces his liver, like a bird darting into a snare, little knowing it will cost him his life.
>
> Now then, my sons, listen to me; pay attention to what I say. Do not let your heart turn to her ways or stray into her paths. Many are the victims she has brought down; her slain are a mighty throng. Her house is a highway to the grave, leading down to the chambers of death. (NIV)

What do you observe in Proverbs 7 about the nature of sexual temptation?

> There is a process of luring and tempting which precedes the man's going into the sin. Notice how the temptress makes the whole thing look very nice and pleasing with no consequences — "My husband is away..." See also: Proverbs 6:23-29.

What is the condition of the man in Proverbs 7:22 after he succumbs to the temptation?

> He is in bondage after he decides to go after the temptress.

Do you detect a conscious plan in the words of the temptress? If so, what do you see that indicates a plan?

> Yes, she seduces the man with seductive speech.

What is the ultimate goal planned for the man?	Death and Sheol.
The traps that are put before us are not random but are part of a larger strategy to hinder our spiritual growth in Christ and ruin our lives and testimonies. Although the temptations often come in human form, there are invisible forces at work behind the scenes.	

Ephesians 6:10-12

> Finally, be strong in the Lord and in his mighty power. Put on the full armor of God so that you can take your stand against the devil's schemes. For our struggle is not against flesh and blood, but against the rulers, against the authorities, against the powers of this dark world and against the spiritual forces of evil in the heavenly realms. (NIV)

What word does the above passage use to describe the devil's work?	A scheme that we are told to stand firm against. A scheme is a plot or a plan. It is the strategy a general may have when preparing to fight a battle.
According to Ephesians 6:12, against whom do we struggle?	Spiritual forces of darkness. This shows there is a demonic dimension to our struggle.

 **pplication** **Allow 20 Minutes**

In the gospels and Revelation, spiritual conflict is a common theme. When Christ came in a physical body to live among us, conflict was evident throughout his earthly life. It was present all the time, and at times it was visibly violent. War on evil is a common theme throughout the Book of Revelation, and the war is exceedingly violent.

In our personal battles with sexual sin, we need to be alert to the component that Satan is intentional in his attacks.

Does knowing that our struggles with sexual temptations (as well as other types) are more than the results of physical desires make any difference in how you will approach overcoming this battle? Briefly explain.	Personal responses.

Facilitator's Guide: *Crossroads*, Turning Point, P. O. Box 22127, Chattanooga, TN 37422-2127

We have thought about the patterns that have been set in our lives and how Satan uses them. Now let's begin to think about a plan to respond to the temptations in these areas.

Imagine that we are about to engage in a military campaign. What work do you think should be done before the fighting begins to help ensure our victory?

The intelligence work—the spying out the enemy and knowing his methods. Standing firm against the schemes of the devil includes being aware of his tactics and methods. The logistic work—knowing our resources and making sure they are in place. Many other responses are possible.

Read 1 Corinthians 6:18.

> Flee from sexual immorality. All other sins a man commits are outside his body, but he who sins sexually sins against his own body. (NIV)

What strategy are we told to use to respond to the temptation of sexual sin?

Sexual sin is the one sin we are told to run from.

We cannot stand nose-to-nose with this temptation. The truth God gives us is flight, but we must still fight our attacker with the weapons we have as we withdraw. That is why we must be clothed with the armor of God—prepared to fight as we withdraw.

Read Ephesians 6:13-18.

> Therefore put on the full armor of God, so that when the day of evil comes, you may be able to stand your ground, and after you have done everything, to stand. Stand firm then, with the belt of truth buckled around your waist, with the breastplate of righteousness in place, and with your feet fitted with the readiness that comes from the gospel of peace. In addition to all this, take up the shield of faith, with which you can extinguish all the flaming arrows of the evil one. Take the helmet of salvation and the sword of the Spirit, which is the word of God. And pray in the Spirit on all occasions with all kinds of prayers and requests. With this in mind, be alert and always keep on praying for all the saints. (NIV)

Identify each component of the "full armor of God" and discuss the significance of each part in our spiritual battle.

Girded loins with TRUTH—girding keeps you from tripping over your robes, and truth speaks against falsehood. Lies trip us up, but truth makes us surefooted. (See also John 17:17 and Romans 12:2.)

Breastplate of RIGHTEOUSNESS—protects our vital organs and is not our righteousness but the righteousness of Christ (Philippians 3:9). We are depending on His saving work, not our own works. This defends against the lies that accuse us.

Feet shod with the preparation of the GOSPEL OF PEACE—this protects our ability to walk and run. The gospel of peace reminds us of the fact that we have peace with God (Romans 5:1), can serve him, and take the battle forward.

Shield of FAITH—deflects (extinguishes) all the flaming darts. (*By faith the mighty saints prevailed...* See Hebrews 11.)

Helmet of SALVATION—protects the most vital part of us. Salvation covers us! Note also we are to have the "mind of Christ" (1 Corinthians 2:16) and "take every thought captive" (2 Corinthians 10:5). We are transformed by the renewing of the mind (Romans 12:1-2).

Sword of the SPIRIT—the only offensive weapon. Satan cannot stand against God's Word. Note the temptation of Jesus in the wilderness and how he used Scripture to defend himself (Luke 4:1-13). We are also told that the Word is a sword that cuts deeply (Hebrews 4:12).

WITH PRAYER—all of this only works when we are praying—getting the support we must have from God. We cannot stand alone. We are to be continually praying (1 Thessalonians 5:17).

Read Hebrews 10:24-25.

> And let us consider how we may spur one another on toward love and good deeds. Let us not give up meeting together, as some are in the habit of doing, but let us encourage one another—and all the more as you see the Day approaching. (NIV)

Read Ecclesiastes 4:9-12.

> Two are better than one, because they have a good return for their work: If one falls down, his friend can help him up. But pity the man who falls and has no one to help him up! Also, if two lie down together, they will keep warm. But how can one keep warm alone? Though one may be overpowered, two can defend themselves. A cord of three strands is not quickly broken. (NIV)

How can you incorporate the truth in the verses we just read into your plan for finding victory over sexual temptation?

We need other people to encourage us, hold us accountable, pray for us, strengthen us, and defend us in the battles of life.

In 1 John 2:14, the Bible makes a statement about young men.

> I have written to you, fathers, because you know Him who has been from the beginning. I have written to you, young men, because you are strong, and the word of God abides in you, and you have overcome the evil one. (NASB)

How does the passage describe these young men, and do you see a key concept for overcoming the evil one? How can you use this principle this week?

They are described as strong. Being full of the Word of God is a key to overcoming the evil one. Reading, memorizing, and meditating in God's Word will strengthen us for the battle.

Closing Prayer

Pray for strength to withstand the attacks of Satan and thank God for providing his armor.

Session **7** *Dependence Upon God Alone*

Introduction

Opening Prayer

Thank God that he has provided for our every need and for his faithfulness to us in all things.

Sharing Questions

Describe a time you felt totally helpless. What did you do?

Personal response (such as an accident, stay in a hospital, etc.)

Self-Awareness

Allow 20-25 Minutes

NOTE TO FACILITATOR:

Hitting bottom is a common experience, but it takes on different shapes for different people. For some, simply being confronted by their spouses might be enough to cause them to *hit bottom* and seek help. Others may have to be diagnosed with HIV or lose their jobs because of their behavior.

Sexual addiction, as any compulsive sinful behavior, progresses in predictable stages. People begin by experimenting with the behavior; soon it becomes part of their social lives; as time goes on, they become more and more preoccupied with the behavior; and eventually the behavior dominates and controls their lives.

Have you noticed a progression in your own compulsive sinful behavior? Which stage would you place yourself in?

Personal response.

At each stage the pain of the consequences grows more intense until ultimately the person struggling loses something so significant it brings him or her to a place where the consequences of continuing in sexual sin seem unbearable. The pain breaks through the delusion that blinds us to the consequences of our sin and brings us to a place of a decision to seek help.

It is said that a person will not change until the pain of staying the same is greater than the pain that it takes to change.

What brought you to the place where you were willing to seek help?

Personal response.

This place of decision is often called *hitting bottom*. The process of *hitting bottom* is common among those of us who struggle with sexual sins. It seems like a necessary part of the process of restoration. Something has to happen to bring us to the end of ourselves—to break our self-dependence. We will never trust God so long as we trust our own abilities.

Maybe you have just *hit bottom* recently, and that event has driven you to get involved with *Crossroads*. Maybe you *hit bottom* years ago, and that painful memory still pierces your heart. Maybe you have not yet *hit bottom*, and the whole idea of this happening scares you. No matter how anyone feels, the pain of *hitting bottom* is inevitable if a person continues in a pattern of sexual sin.

Describe a time when your sexual sins caused you to hit bottom.

Personal response.

People react to the pain of hitting bottom in two ways. Some are brought to a place of helplessness and look for help to change. Others use the pain as an excuse to sink deeper into addiction.

How do you think God can use the pain that comes from the consequences of our sin to draw us to him?

When we come to a place of despair, we realize how out of control our lives have become. We realize the sinful choices we have made and how we are enslaved to sin. We know something has to change, and we know we cannot do it ourselves. It is only when we reach the end of ourselves and we turn to God that we experience his power to change our lives.

Even great heroes in the Bible had times when they surrendered to temptation. Without exception, they found restoration the same way we do today. They were brought to their senses by the consequences of their sin, which drove them to seek God.

King David had this to say about his guilt over his sin with a woman named Bathsheba:

> For I recognize my shameful deeds—they haunt me day and night.
>
> Against you, and you alone, have I sinned; I have done what is evil in your sight. You will be proved right in what you say, and your judgment against me is just (Psalm 51:3-4 NLT).

What evidence do you see in these verses that King David was brought to a personal *bottom* by his sin? How did he respond?

He could not sleep for thinking about what he had done. He did not excuse himself, and he repented and agreed with God that what he had done was wrong.

Spiritual-Awareness

Allow 20-25 Minutes

Philippians 2:12-13

> Therefore, my dear friends, as you have always obeyed—not only in my presence, but now much more in my absence—continue to work out your salvation with fear and trembling, for it is God who works in you to will and to act according to his good purpose. (NIV)

These verses teach us that we have a responsibility to humbly respond to God as he works in our lives. It is not a casual commitment but one that requires constant attention and dependence upon God.

When we make sinful choices, we announce that we desire to act independent of God.

What motivations do you think are behind our decisions to make sinful choices?

Answers may include: A desire to control our circumstances, to soothe our pains, to still our anxiety, to solve problems without having to depend on anyone else.

As mentioned earlier, the experience of *hitting bottom* brings us to a point of absolute dependence on God because we recognize we cannot rely on ourselves. The experience brings us to the end of our sinful pride.

The fact that God uses the painful consequences of our sinful behaviors to get our attention is sometimes called his *severe mercy*. Disobeying God can bring frightening consequences, as happened in the situations described in the following passages:

Jeremiah 15:1-2

> Then the LORD said to me: "Even if Moses and Samuel were to stand before me, my heart would not go out to this people. Send them away from my presence! Let them go! And if they ask you, 'Where shall we go?' tell them, 'This is what the LORD says: " 'Those destined for death, to death; those for the sword, to the sword; those for starvation, to starvation; those for captivity, to captivity.' (NIV)

The people of Judah had continually turned their backs on God, and finally the time for consequences arrived. God was going to allow the people to feel the impact of choosing to ignore him.

When you read the words in Jeremiah 15:1-2, what emotions come to you?

> Various answers, but likely the group will respond that the words are chilling.

What does this passage tell us about a relationship with God?

> They show us that eventually our rebellion will bring us intense suffering in this life, to say nothing of the life to come.

Romans 1:24-27

> Therefore God gave them over in the sinful desires of their hearts to sexual impurity for the degrading of their bodies with one another. They exchanged the truth of God for a lie, and worshiped and served created things rather than the Creator—who is forever praised. Amen.
>
> Because of this, God gave them over to shameful lusts. Even their women exchanged natural relations for unnatural ones. In the same way the men also abandoned natural relations with women and were inflamed with lust for one another. Men committed indecent acts with other men, and received in themselves the due penalty for their perversion. (NIV)

What natural consequence of sinful choices did God allow to occur in the hearts of the people described in the previous passage?

> God allowed them to lose themselves in their sin and become totally degraded. Without any restraint, they destroy themselves and lose all dignity.

Did these people get off easy, or was this a severe consequence?

> This is a severe consequence of sin, one of the most frightening punishments imaginable because we destroy ourselves and there is nobody to help us.

The passages from Romans and Jeremiah were written about people who were not Christians. They reveal that when God deals with those who reject him, his method is to *let them go*, and their sinful acts contain their own earthly punishment in addition to the eternal punishment to occur after death. This is a frightening fact but one which cannot be ignored.

For Christians, however, a similar dynamic remains regarding our sin and the way God deals with us. God does not take a casual attitude toward sin, and He will bring loving discipline to bear.

One method of discipline—letting a person go in his or her sin—is to hand the person over to Satan for destruction with the intent that the person's soul will be saved. The act of abandonment drives a person to the point of seeing that only God can bring him or her out of the despair and destruction.

1 Corinthians 5:1-5

> I can hardly believe the report about the sexual immorality going on among you, something so evil that even the pagans don't do it. I am told that you have a man in your church who is living in sin with his father's wife. And you are so proud of yourselves! Why aren't you mourning in sorrow and shame? And why haven't you removed this man from your fellowship?
>
> Even though I am not there with you in person, I am with you in the Spirit. Concerning the one who has done this, I have already passed judgment in the name of the Lord Jesus. You are to call a meeting of the church, and I will be there in spirit, and the power of the Lord Jesus will be with you as you meet. Then you must cast this man out of the church and into Satan's hands, so that his sinful nature will be destroyed and he himself will be saved when the Lord returns. (NLT)

Why was the Apostle Paul shocked by the reaction of the Corinthian Christians?

> Because of their casual acceptance of terrible sin.

Facilitator's Guide: *Crossroads*, Turning Point, P. O. Box 22127, Chattanooga, TN 37422-2127

In your opinion, is the act of turning this man out of the church motivated by love or vengeance? Why?

Personal response.

Hebrews 12:4-13

After all, you have not yet given your lives in your struggle against sin. And have you entirely forgotten the encouraging words God spoke to you, his children? He said,

"My child, don't ignore it when the Lord disciplines you, and don't be discouraged when he corrects you. For the Lord disciplines those he loves, and he punishes those he accepts as his children."

As you endure this divine discipline, remember that God is treating you as his own children. Whoever heard of a child who was never disciplined? If God doesn't discipline you as he does all of his children, it means that you are illegitimate and are not really his children after all. Since we respect our earthly fathers who disciplined us, should we not all the more cheerfully submit to the discipline of our heavenly Father and live forever?

For our earthly fathers disciplined us for a few years, doing the best they knew how. But God's discipline is always right and good for us because it means we will share in his holiness. No discipline is enjoyable while it is happening—it is painful! But afterward there will be a quiet harvest of right living for those who are trained in this way.

So take a new grip with your tired hands and stand firm on your shaky legs. Mark out a straight path for your feet. Then those who follow you, though they are weak and lame, will not stumble and fall but will become strong. (NLT)

Many people in our culture have come to associate discipline with vengeance, but true discipline is an act of love.

How have you experienced God's corrective discipline in your life? What was the outcome?

Personal response.

As much as we would like to think otherwise, every act of disobedience to God produces consequences. We may not recognize them immediately, but over a period of time, their impact is unmistakable. This principle of sowing an action and reaping the consequences or benefits is described for us in Galatians.

Galatians 6:7-9

Do not be deceived: God cannot be mocked. A man reaps what he sows. The one who sows to please his sinful nature, from that nature will reap destruction; the one who sows to please the

Spirit, from the Spirit will reap eternal life. Let us not become weary in doing good, for at the proper time we will reap a harvest if we do not give up. (NIV)

How do you think we deceive ourselves when we choose to engage in sexual sin?

> We rationalize our behavior, we excuse our behavior, we tell ourselves it is not hurting anyone, we pretend that God does not see, and many other responses.

Think about this concept of sowing and reaping. What ideas do you have as to why this is a good picture of the consequences of choosing to disobey God?

> Some responses include: You generally reap much more than you sow; the seed is small, but the resulting plant is much larger; you cannot control the growth of the plant, it happens naturally, etc. Generally the consequence of sowing is way out of proportion to the act of planting.

We can see in these passages that if we continue in disobedience, the consequences will eventually become so severe that we are brought back to our senses and understand that we can do nothing apart from God's grace working in our lives.

Application

Allow 20 Minutes

After looking at the issue that God holds us all accountable for our actions and that there are consequences attached to our sinful disobedience, it would be easy to feel that we are in a hopeless situation. Who can lead a life of perfect obedience?

This is why it is important to understand that God does not accept us because of our perfect performance in always pleasing him. We are acceptable to him because of his grace and the sacrifice of his Son in our place.

Read Ephesians 2:8-10:

> For it is by grace you have been saved, through faith—and this not from yourselves, it is the gift of God— not by works, so that no one can boast. For we are God's workmanship, created in Christ Jesus to do good works, which God prepared in advance for us to do. (NIV)

How would you define grace?

In your opinion, how does experiencing *the bottom* prepare us for God's grace?

Is there anything we can do to make ourselves less dependent upon God for our salvation?

This passage speaks of those who have been saved as being God's *workmanship* or *masterpiece.* Regardless of how we may feel at any moment about ourselves, if we are believers, we are precious because of what God has done for us. All creation is in awe of the love and grace God has shown to rebellious humans.

A masterpiece does not create itself. Someone has to do the work that others look at and admire. A masterpiece is placed in a gallery for onlookers to admire and praise the creator. We are on display in the gallery of life. The world is watching.

According to Ephesians 2:8-10, what purpose do we have in life?

Is it possible to fulfill that purpose without total dependence on God?

How are you showing dependence on God now?

Grace is an undeserved gift, unmerited pay. It is something that comes from God when we do not desire it. It is not of our own creation or work.

It is by *hitting bottom* that we come to the point where we recognize that we cannot help ourselves. If we are to get help, it has to be a supernatural act of God that can only be realized by trusting in God and God alone. When we realize our helplessness, we are in a position to trust in God's grace.

There is nothing, absolutely nothing that we contribute. Salvation is a result of God's grace and nothing else. We cannot be "saved" from our sins—in general—or our sin in particular without grace. The problem with God and his grace is that we cannot control, manipulate, or force it—instead, we have to accept what he gives when he gives.

We are created in Christ Jesus to do good works, which God prepared in advance for us to do.

We are powerless without God at work in our lives.

Personal response.

Closing Prayer

Thank God that he accepts us on the basis of his grace and not because of our perfect obedience. Pray that our lives will bring glory to him as we display his workmanship.

Facilitator's Guide: *Crossroads*, Turning Point, P. O. Box 22127, Chattanooga, TN 37422-2127

Session 8 — Be Holy Because I Am Holy

Introduction

Allow 10 Minutes

Opening Prayer

| | Ask God to reveal to the group the truth of his holiness and to create in each member a healthy fear of God. |

Sharing Questions

What is the most compelling reason you have for fighting against your addictive sexual behaviors?

Personal response.

Self-Awareness

Allow 20-25 Minutes

NOTE TO FACILITATOR:

The key idea of this lesson is that if our core motive is anything other than being holy because God is holy, then we will not have adequate reasons to avoid sin. For example, if we choose not to sin because of an even deeper sinful motivation—fear of man—then even though the lustful sin may be avoided, the individual is still operating out of sin and this is fatal.

It is important not only to learn *how* to do something, but also *why* it is you do what you do. When teaching children mathematics, there is an inclination to tell them what to do and not to worry about the *why*. Yet when they move from one function of math to another, if they do not understand the reasoning *why* certain things are done, they will be confused and possibly make errors. For example, when my children were learning how to carry tens when adding columns of numbers, they were fine so long as it only involved a "1." They knew that you always would carry the "1," but they did not know it represented a ten; so when they ran into carrying "twenty," they did not know how to handle it.

There is more to the struggle of sanctification against sexual sin than just knowing *what* to do and when to do it. Just as we can program robots but when a new situation comes at them, they shut down, we have to be ready to respond to the unexpected. This requires more than simply learning a system of things to do. If we do not have the proper motivation, we will be vulnerable to failure in "new" situations. There will come a time when all the methods that are discussed in these sessions seem to fail due to the peculiarities of the situation. If a person is totally dependent on his accountability partner and the partner is away on vacation, what then?

Describe an experience when you were vulnerable because you faced an unexpected situation or temptation.

Personal response.

Added to this problem is the fact that when we are dealing with sin issues, the motives of our hearts are critical. The Bible reminds us that our hearts are deceitful beyond all things and we are prone to lie to ourselves. We rationalize what we do and because of this, it is often hard for us to see clearly what is right and wrong. We can find ways around all our reasons to obey God. We can find excuses *not* to apply the methods we learn to battle our sin, and even when we obey God, we may be doing it for the wrong reason. Jesus stated in Matthew 5:27-28 that we are judged not only according to our actions but also according to our motives.

Spiritual Awareness Lead-In

Read 1 Corinthians 4:3-5.

What about me? Have I been faithful? Well, it matters very little what you or anyone else thinks. I don't even trust my own judgment on this point. My conscience is clear, but that isn't what matters. It is the Lord himself who will examine me and decide. So be careful not to jump to conclusions before the Lord returns as to whether or not someone is faithful. When the Lord comes, he will bring our deepest secrets to light and will reveal our private motives. And then God will give to everyone whatever praise is due. (NLT)

In light of this verse, why should we be careful in evaluating our level of spiritual commitment?

Personal response.

When will the truth be known?

Personal response.

How does this make you feel?

Personal response.

The passage in 1 Corinthians 4:3-5 makes it clear that our private motives will one day be brought to light and these motives will be judged. We tend to judge one another by actions that we can observe, but when it comes to judging the motivations behind those actions, our ability is very limited. As the Apostle Paul said in the passage we just read, he did not trust even his own self-evaluation.

Take a few minutes and list as many motivations and reasons that you can think of for not pursuing sexual sin.

This should be done as an exercise, perhaps using a blackboard or overhead. Make a list of reasons participants might avoid sinning. This list will probably include such things as fear of being seen, fear of losing their jobs, fear of AIDS or other STDs, fear of their spouses finding out, fear of divorce, thinking it is a waste of time, and knowing they will feel terrible afterwards.

What is a common factor among these?

The reasons which focus on consequences dealing with reputation, etc., tend to be based on a deeper core sin of "fearing man." The Bible speaks against our living our lives as "man-pleasers" like the Pharisees who were righteous in behavior but for the wrong reasons. The reasons that focus on consequences dealing with sickness and death may seem to be based on a "fear of God" but upon analysis are really rooted in a selfish heart. "I do not want something to happen to me....If I knew I would not have to experience consequences and am supposed to obey simply because God wants me to, I will not..."

Jeremiah 17:9

> The heart is deceitful above all things and beyond cure. Who can understand it? (NIV)

This often-quoted verse summarizes the difficulty we have in understanding our own motivations.

In light of this fact, what can we expect to happen if we are in situations where we can rationalize away the fear of man or the fear of consequences?

Since our hearts are deceitful, we know we have a tendency to lie even to ourselves. We can rationalize most anything. Therefore, if our reasons are based on fears of consequences, we will reason them away. Example: "I know this woman. She is clean; I do not have to fear AIDS. We are shrewd, and no one will ever catch us..."

Proverbs 1:7; 9:10-12

The fear of the LORD is the beginning of knowledge; Fools despise wisdom and instruction. (NASB)

The fear of the LORD is the beginning of wisdom, and the knowledge of the Holy One is understanding. For by me your days will be multiplied, And years of life will be added to you. If you are wise, you are wise for yourself, And if you scoff, you alone will bear it. (NASB)

According to these verses, what great benefit derives from fearing God? Why do you think this is so?

Wisdom is born from our fear of God. When we understand that God judges impartially according to his absolute standards and not our confused notions of right and wrong, then we begin to see clearly and make good decisions.

Define in your own words *the fear of God.* Be prepared to discuss your definition with the group.

Not simply respect — The Hebrew word means "terror" and the Greek word used to translate it is *phobos* from which we get our word phobia, which means fear. It is more than respect. It is fear of. It is like the terror we might feel before a raging storm over which we have no control.

As we have seen, it is clear that the beginning of wisdom is "fear of God."

How can this fear motivate us to make right choices and drive us to depend upon God?

If you never fear God, you will never turn from your sin. Until you see him as absolutely holy and righteous as well as the Creator—knowing that he does not wink at sin—you will try to slide by. Until you realize that without his grace you are doomed, you will not turn to him for help.

Facilitator's Guide: *Crossroads,* Turning Point, P. O. Box 22127, Chattanooga, TN 37422-2127

We can have a fearful respect for someone or something when we realize the potential that person or thing has to destroy us, even if it does not. If you experience a near miss with a tractor-trailer truck, you certainly experience fear and are grateful you were spared. When we realize that if it were not for the grace of God, we would be doomed, then we can be both fearful and thankful at the same time. Imagine what it would be like if God did not choose to save people!

Fear as a motivator has an important place in God's plan, but he desires much more for us than a cowering submission, always fearing punishment.

1 John 4:17-19

> Love is made complete among us so that we will have confidence on the day of judgment, because in this world we are like him. There is no fear in love. But perfect love drives out fear, because fear has to do with punishment. The one who fears is not made perfect in love. We love because he first loved us. (NIV)

According to your understanding of this verse, how can perfect love drive out fear?

When we see what God has done for us, we do not have to fear the judgment.

How do you think obeying God motivated by fear differs from obeying God motivated by love?

If I realize how much God loves me, then my loving response is to be obedient to him. My motive becomes one of wanting to show my love for God. My motive becomes "God-centered."

To us, love and fear seem to be opposites—and one cannot coexist with the other. Many people have trouble with the tension they feel when trying to balance two truths that seem to work against each other. Because these paradoxes are so common in the Bible, it is important that we are able to hold two truths in balance. If we abandon one and overemphasize the other, the result is a distorted view of the Christian life. In order to achieve balance, we must hold on to both at the same time.

1 Peter 1:13-17

Therefore, prepare your minds for action; be self-controlled; set your hope fully on the grace to be given you when Jesus Christ is revealed. As obedient children, do not conform to the evil desires you had when you lived in ignorance. But just as he who called you is holy, so be holy in all you do; for it is written: "Be holy, because I am holy."

Since you call on a Father who judges each man's work impartially, live your lives as strangers here in reverent fear. (NIV)

In this passage, we are told to "be holy in all we do; for it is written: 'Be holy, because I am holy.'"

What commands are given in the verses prior to this statement?

Prepare your minds for action, be self-controlled, set your hope fully on the grace we will receive when Christ returns, do not conform to evil desires.

How would making these commands a priority in our lives facilitate being holy in all we do?

Following these commands will make us aware every moment of our love for and dependency upon God and will facilitate our becoming more like God.

The last verse of the passage instructs us to live our lives as people who are just passing through this life and to hold a reverent fear of God. As we considered earlier in this session, most people are more moved by the fear of man and the fear of consequences than by the fear of God.

In what ways can you see that being motivated by the fear and love of God is superior to other motivations?

Our eyes are moved off of ourselves and onto God. Instead of thinking in a self-oriented (self-centered) fashion, we are drawn out of ourselves. Selfishness is the core cause of sin, so any selfish motive only makes matters worse. The God-oriented motive makes a big difference.

What ways can you see that living your life motivated by a healthy fear of God and pursuit of holiness will help you deal with your deceitful heart spoken of in Jeremiah 17:9?

The deceitful heart can rationalize around all our excuses not to sin, but the deceitful heart cannot get around the FACT of God's holiness. God is unchanging. He is a perfect standard. When we are confronted by the ultimate motive—"Be holy because I am holy"—we cannot reason that God is not holy.

Facilitator's Guide: *Crossroads*, Turning Point, P. O. Box 22127, Chattanooga, TN 37422-2127

We may pursue sexual sin for many reasons, but at the core is a determination to satisfy selfish desires without regard for God's law. We seem to have an unlimited ability to excuse our actions because our hearts are deceitful.

When it comes to quitting our compulsive sexual behavior, we will have to examine our motives if we are to overcome our besetting sin and live a life that is pleasing to God. Our motive must be deeper than the fear of contracting a disease or being exposed. These motives may restrain us temporarily, but we will eventually find many excuses to return to our old habits.

It all eventually comes down to answering this question: Why do I want to quit my sin? If the "why" is because we have a healthy fear of God and an understanding of his love and we want to live a life that is holy as he is holy, then we have the foundation built to have greater victory over our sins. Our response of love, strengthened by our desire to be holy for one reason only—because God is holy, will enable us to actually have greater victory over our sins. The right reason gives strength for right behavior.

Think deeply about your own life and prepare to share with the group some of your personal motivations for not pursuing sexual sin.

Personal response.

Have some of these motivations been more helpful than others?

Personal response.

When faced with a temptation, which do you think will be more helpful to you: (1) A list of rules and procedures you should follow or (2) a healthy fear of God and an understanding of his love? Explain briefly.

Personal response.

We might be able to come up with specific methods to avoid particular sins, but the tempter is very creative in coming up with variations and new approaches to tempt us. While our methods may work well in one situation, they may not be right for another. The ultimate motive of God's holiness is unchanging and effective for any temptation. No matter what temptations come at us, we know God's standard of holiness does not change.

Closing Prayer

Lead the group in a time of prayerful meditation through the following topics. Encourage group members to pray aloud as they consider:

- God's holiness.

- Our sin.

- Our need to repent.

- Our thankfulness for His forgiveness in Christ.

- The price God paid for our forgiveness.

- Our desire to have our motives be godly motives.

Facilitator's Guide: *Crossroads*, Turning Point, P. O. Box 22127, Chattanooga, TN 37422-2127

Session 9 Renewing the Mind

Introduction

Allow 10 Minutes

Opening Prayer

Ask God for help to value the things he values.

Sharing Questions

How did you do adjusting your motivations based on the last session?

Personal response.

Self-Awareness

Allow 20-25 Minutes

NOTE TO FACILITATOR:

The point behind this session is based on an argument Jonathan Edwards made that even when we choose to do things we know are wrong, we do them because we believe them to be beneficial. We may choose to sin because we are convinced it is better to sin and have the present pleasure than to obey and have to endure the pain. We believe the relief of the pain is important enough to justify the sin. When we fall into this trap, a behavior cycle can become established where our concept of right and wrong is distorted by our desire to avoid the pain of doing what is right.

Jonathan Edwards, whose ministry led the way in a revival commonly known as the "Great Awakening," was a brilliant American theologian and philosopher who lived during the early 1700s. Edwards made the following statement: "We always choose what we believe is most beneficial." By this, he meant we are convinced that it is better to sin and have present pleasure than to obey and endure the pain.

This type of thinking process always leads to making wrong choices. These choices develop into patterns of behaviors that become part of our lifestyles—lifestyles that are not pleasing to God.

The New Testament ties our ability to make personal change to the process of a change that occurs in our thought life. This process of change is described as the renewing (or "again-new-ing") of our minds.

This process of change is often called sanctification. The Latin word from which sanctification comes is *sanctus*, which means holy. It is the root word of other holy-related words like sanctuary and sanctum. The Greek word behind the Latin is *hagios*, which also means holy. When Jesus says in John 17:17, "Sanctify them. . . ," He is saying, "Holify them — make them holy."

Sanctification is the growth in Christ we experience as believers wherein we are slowly changed from who we are in our sinful natures to who we are declared to be in Christ. In Christ we are new creations. In Christ we are forgiven, and no longer does God look upon us as sinners in rebellion against him. Yet our flesh still lives within us, and our lives are constant battles against our sinful desires. Paul discusses these struggles in Romans 7:15-25:

> I do not understand what I do. For what I want to do I do not do, but what I hate I do. And if I do what I do not want to do, I agree that the law is good. As it is, it is no longer I myself who do it, but it is sin living in me. I know that nothing good lives in me, that is, in my sinful nature. For I have the desire to do what is good, but I cannot carry it out. For what I do is not the good I want to do; no, the evil I do not want to do—this I keep on doing. Now if I do what I do not want to do, it is no longer I who do it, but it is sin living in me that does it.
>
> So I find this law at work: When I want to do good, evil is right there with me. For in my inner being I delight in God's law; but I see another law at work in the members of my body, waging war against the law of my mind and making me a prisoner of the law of sin at work within my members. What a wretched man I am! Who will rescue me from this body of death? Thanks be to God—through Jesus Christ our Lord.
>
> So then, I myself in my mind am a slave to God's law, but in the sinful nature a slave to the law of sin. (NIV)

Do the words of Romans 7:15-25 describe how you feel in your struggle with sexual impurity? Explain.

It is important that while this concept be discussed so that participants can understand that their perceptions of right and wrong have been twisted by their use of porn and other sexual sins to get gratification, it is also important that the discussion not get mired down in the "philosophy" of the question. It might be best to focus on individuals' accounts of choices they have made rationalizing them to be right.

Some people have the misperception that when they become Christians, they will no longer have to struggle with sinful urges. As shown in the passage above, even mature Christians must deal with the sinful nature that works against our being the people we want to be—people whose lives please God.

Facilitator's Guide: *Crossroads*, Turning Point, P. O. Box 22127, Chattanooga, TN 37422-2127

So how does God change us? Jesus says, "Sanctify them with truth, Your Word is truth"(John 17:17). This means that God makes us holy by the application of his Word to us. The way this works is that God alters our mind-sets and changes our inner value system. He creates in us a new way of thinking and therefore a new way of desiring and doing, as described in Philippians 2:12-13:

> Dearest friends, you were always so careful to follow my instructions when I was with you. And now that I am away you must be even more careful to put into action God's saving work in your lives, obeying God with deep reverence and fear. For God is working in you, giving you the desire to obey him and the power to do what pleases him. (NLT)

God works in us through the Holy Spirit who supernaturally gives us the desire to obey God and the power to do what pleases him. This is further emphasized in Romans 8:5-9:

> Those who are dominated by the sinful nature think about sinful things, but those who are controlled by the Holy Spirit think about things that please the Spirit. If your sinful nature controls your mind, there is death. But if the Holy Spirit controls your mind, there is life and peace. For the sinful nature is always hostile to God. It never did obey God's laws, and it never will. That's why those who are still under the control of their sinful nature can never please God.

> But you are not controlled by your sinful nature. You are controlled by the Spirit if you have the Spirit of God living in you. (And remember that those who do not have the Spirit of Christ living in them are not Christians at all.) (NLT)

For years we have lived lives where we have valued things that are against God's will. We have desired sinful things such as immoral sexual relations or fantasies about such things. We have allowed pornography and other sexual sins to encourage us to place a great value upon sexual fulfillment. We have raised up our sexual fulfillment as an idol. These thoughts and desires have been "burned" into our very neural pathways, and often we sin out of habit and without much forethought. It should be clear that in order to change our behavior, God must first change our values; and in order to change our values, he must first change our minds and hearts, which is the work of the Spirit in us. This concept is critical to us, and we need to discuss its implications—both in why we sin and in how we can stop.

Spiritual Awareness Lead–In

When you began to choose to walk the path leading to sexual impurity, did you have to ignore your conscience and harden your heart to continue activities that you knew were wrong?

When we resist the conviction God brings to our hearts that what we are doing is wrong, we will justify our actions with many excuses or pretend that what we are doing does not matter.

If so, how did you justify your choice?

Personal response.

What were the consequences?

The consequence was that we no longer could recognize the truth and we became more unfeeling.

Spiritual-Awareness

Allow 20-25 Minutes

Before we look at the Bible passages that discuss how we are changed as a Christian, it is important to evaluate ourselves to be sure that we are born again. Until we are, any change that we accomplish will only have temporary value instead of eternal benefit.

Many metaphors are used to describe the Christian life—a journey, an adventure, a pilgrimage—but no matter which metaphors you choose, there is still an element of mystery and wonder in how God chooses us to be his own.

    Facilitator's Guide: *Crossroads,* Turning Point, P. O. Box 22127, Chattanooga, TN 37422-2127

John 3:3-8

Jesus replied, "I assure you, unless you are born again, you can never see the Kingdom of God."

"What do you mean?" exclaimed Nicodemus. "How can an old man go back into his mother's womb and be born again?"

Jesus replied, "The truth is, no one can enter the Kingdom of God without being born of water and the Spirit. Humans can reproduce only human life, but the Holy Spirit gives new life from heaven. So don't be surprised at my statement that you must be born again. Just as you can hear the wind but can't tell where it comes from or where it is going, so you can't explain how people are born of the Spirit." (NLT)

In the above passage, Nicodemus—a man very familiar with the Jewish religion—is mystified by the concept of being born again. Jesus explains to him that he must be (the literal translation is) *born from above.*

What evidence do you see in the passage that being born again is a supernatural work of God?

> Jesus explains to Nicodemus that being "born from above" is not humanly possible; it is a supernatural event.

According to Jesus, is the new birth something we can fully explain?

> Just as it is impossible to see the wind or predict its path (without special instruments), it is impossible to explain how people are born of the Spirit.

Later in the same chapter Jesus says:

For God so loved the world that he gave his only Son, so that everyone who believes in him will not perish but have eternal life. God did not send his Son into the world to condemn it, but to save it (John 3:16-17 NLT).

Be prepared to share with the group your experience of the new birth if you have been born again.

> There may be those in the group who have never been born again. Take time to explain to them how a person can respond to God's call by faith.

Ezekiel 11:19-20

> I will give them an undivided heart and put a new spirit in them; I will remove from them their heart of stone and give them a heart of flesh. Then they will follow my decrees and be careful to keep my laws. They will be my people, and I will be their God. (NIV)

This Bible passage also describes what happens to us when we are born again.

What is the result of God's giving us an undivided heart and putting a new spirit in us?

This passage describes how God will work in a person who turns to him. He will form within that person a desire to please him as described by the words, "I will remove from them their heart of stone and give them a heart of flesh."

A good indicator that we have been born again is the desire we receive to follow God's will and to enjoy fellowship with him. When we sin, we have a deep conviction that we have grieved God. To continue in sin requires that we once again harden our heart to the conviction that God brings to us through his Spirit.

It is possible for some people to change their behaviors without coming to Christ, but the problem is that often people will exchange one addiction for another. An alcoholic may quit drinking, but then to medicate the pain in his life he was covering with alcohol may develop a sexual addiction.

We are interested in more than just stopping a self-destructive behavior. We are interested in growing in a relationship with the God who has given us a new heart. The behavior will change as we grow closer to God, and we will also have the benefit of knowing our lifestyle is bringing glory to God.

Romans 12:1-2

> Therefore I urge you, brethren, by the mercies of God, to present your bodies a living and holy sacrifice, acceptable to God, which is your spiritual service of worship. And do not be conformed to this world, but be transformed by the renewing of your mind, so that you may prove what the will of God is, that which is good and acceptable and perfect. (NASB)

Facilitator's Guide: *Crossroads*, Turning Point, P. O. Box 22127, Chattanooga, TN 37422-2127

What three commands in these verses are we urged to obey?	Present our bodies a living and holy sacrifice; do not be conformed to this world; be transformed by the renewing of our minds.
According to these verses, what is the secret to being transformed from conformity with the world?	Having our minds renewed.
Be prepared to discuss specific actions you might take in order to obey these commands.	Allow the group to brainstorm here. This will be discussed more in the Application section of the group.

Ephesians 4:20-24

> But you did not learn Christ in this way, if indeed you have heard Him and have been taught in Him, just as truth is in Jesus, that, in reference to your former manner of life, you lay aside the old self, which is being corrupted in accordance with the lusts of deceit, and that you be renewed in the spirit of your mind, and put on the new self, which in the likeness of God has been created in righteousness and holiness of the truth. (NASB)

According to these verses, what is the secret to laying aside the old self?	Being renewed in the spirit of our minds.

Colossians 3:9-10

> Do not lie to one another, since you laid aside the old self with its evil practices, and have put on the new self who is being renewed to a true knowledge according to the image of the One who created him. (NASB)

According to these verses, what is happening to the new self that we are instructed to put on?	The new self is being renewed to a true knowledge that conforms to the image of God.

Colossians 3:1-3

> Therefore, if then you have been raised up with Christ, keep seeking the things above, where Christ is, seated at the right hand of God. Set your mind on the things above, not on the things that are on earth. For you have died and your life is hidden with Christ in God. (NASB)

What advice can you find in these verses to help in your quest to renew your mind?

Keep thinking of the things of God.

pplication

Allow 20 Minutes

It should be obvious from this lesson—and others—that without the regeneration of the Holy Spirit, we cannot hope for any true change in our lives. At best, we will switch addictions and maybe find a less destructive idol—though this will still lead to eternal damnation. We each must search our hearts to see if we are saved. If you have any doubts about this, cry out to the Holy Spirit to come to you and enable you to believe. (This very action may very well be evidence that you already are regenerate.)

Assuming that you are saved, then you need to implement the truths of this lesson into your life. You need to find ways to study and memorize the Word of God. You need to find a good church where grace is preached and the Bible is taught faithfully. You need to find someone to help keep you accountable according to God's Word. You may even need to locate a good Christian counselor to help you apply the Word of God to your heart issues. In the midst of all this, however, do not trust in your own abilities to do these tasks. Whenever we become self-reliant, we set ourselves up for a fall. We are saved by grace, and we live by grace.

How has using pornography or engaging in immoral sexual acts slowly altered your sense of right and wrong?

Encourage members to be specific about how this change occurred. The main point to focus on is how the mind is altered in what it thinks is right or wrong and it is out of this "belief system" that we act.

It has been said that our thoughts result in decisions, our decisions translate into actions, our actions grow into habits, our habits define our character, and our character determines our destiny.

If this is true and we want to change our lifestyles, where do you think we should concentrate our attention in our effort to change?

Listed below are some practical actions that we can take to help us in renewing our minds to a place where we can once again function with an accurate sense of what is right and wrong.

- Daily reading and study of God's Word

- Regular attendance at church where the Bible is believed and taught

- Having friends who know you and your struggles and who care enough about you to hold you accountable

- Memorizing sections of the Bible to help us overcome Satan's temptations

- Seeking help from a Christian counselor who can help us examine our thoughts and beliefs and then correct them according to the Word of God

- Singing praises to God for his mercy and grace

- Meditating on the Scriptures through the course of a day

- Keeping our minds disciplined to think on things that are honorable, right, pure, lovely, of good report, true, excellent, and worthy of praise (Philippians 4:8)

- Making a covenant to guard our eyes from lust (Job 31:1)

- Being filled with the Spirit (Ephesians 5:18)

The one place that has an impact on all the other areas is our thought life.

What actions would you add to this list?

Personal responses.

What is your plan to cultivate a renewed mind?

Have each member share his or her action plan to cultivate a renewed mind; and if they so choose, ask for other members to hold him or her accountable for following the plan.

Closing Prayer

Ask God for the ability to carry out the action plans the group members have described.

Facilitator's Guide: *Crossroads*, Turning Point, P. O. Box 22127, Chattanooga, TN 37422-2127

Session 10 Natural vs. Normal

Introduction

Allow 10 Minutes

Opening Prayer

> Ask God to give group members the ability to say "no" to selfish desires and to say "yes" to trusting God to fulfill our needs.

Sharing Questions

Describe a temptation you experienced last week and how you responded.

> Personal response.

Self-Awareness

Allow 20-25 Minutes

> NOTE TO FACILITATOR:
>
> This lesson is a straightforward look at how Jesus dealt with temptation. The main focus is to see that He was tempted in the same way that we are—to do things on His own. He was tempted to "take matters into His own hands." We can learn from Jesus how do deal with these exact same types of temptations by yielding to God through a proper understanding of his Word.

Everyone experiences natural needs and desires that are, in themselves, not sinful. They are a natural part of human existence.

Have the group name as many of these natural desires as occur to them.

> Responses will include: hunger, thirst, security, love, comfort, sex, power, control, shelter, and many others. Personal responses.

It is common in the post-Christian thinking of our time to assume that a human being is just another animal and that when we make decisions to satisfy our needs and desires—no matter how we choose to satisfy ourselves—we are not morally responsible for our choices. For example, some researchers will observe homosexual activities among apes and say that since such activity occurs naturally among a species similar to ours, it is only natural to accept such behavior in humans. Or they may say that since the success of many species in nature is due to the strongest males mating with as many females as possible, it is only natural to accept that the human male will be promiscuous.

What are other arguments you have heard or used to justify sexual immorality?

Personal responses.

What argument(s) can you come up with to counter the justification of sin by people who say: It's only natural, so why should I be held responsible?

There are many arguments the group will suggest. One could be that since we have a natural desire to achieve power and success and because in the natural world this is usually achieved by the stronger victimizing the weaker, then it is only natural to accept that the thief who mugs a person or the dishonest broker who cheats his client should not be held responsible for his actions. It is just the law of the jungle.

There is a great distinction between what is "natural" and what is "normal" for a Christian. For our discussion here, we will define those desires and needs that are "natural" as belonging to our "old self"; that is, to the person we were before we were born again. We will define those desires that are "normal" as belonging to our "new self"; the person we became when God gave us new life in Christ.

Spiritual Awareness Lead–In

Every moment of life we are influenced by our needs and desires. Every choice we make is a choice that takes into consideration the potential to satisfy our needs and desires. Some religions seek a place where physical desires disappear, but the Christian life calls us to be motivated by a desire for achieving a "normal" life where our needs and desires come under the lordship of Christ—not one that is just "natural" where the gratification of natural desires is the highest priority. We are called to a life motivated and empowered by the Spirit of God.

Ask the group to read Galatians 5:19-25.

When you follow the desires of your sinful nature, your lives will produce these evil results: sexual immorality, impure thoughts, eagerness for lustful pleasure, idolatry, participation in demonic activities, hostility, quarreling, jealousy, outbursts of anger, selfish ambition, divisions, the feeling that everyone is wrong except those in your own little group, envy,

Facilitator's Guide: *Crossroads*, Turning Point, P. O. Box 22127, Chattanooga, TN 37422-2127

drunkenness, wild parties, and other kinds of sin. Let me tell you again, as I have before, that anyone living that sort of life will not inherit the Kingdom of God.

But when the Holy Spirit controls our lives, he will produce this kind of fruit in us: love, joy, peace, patience, kindness, goodness, faithfulness, gentleness, and self-control. Here there is no conflict with the law.

Those who belong to Christ Jesus have nailed the passions and desires of their sinful nature to his cross and crucified them there. If we are living now by the Holy Spirit, let us follow the Holy Spirit's leading in every part of our lives. (NLT)

Which of these behaviors would you consider "natural" and which would you consider "normal"? Why?

Natural = the desires of the sinful nature
Normal = the fruit of the Spirit

What does this passage tell us we need to know if we are to fulfill our "normal" desires?

Crucify our destructive natural desires and follow the Holy Spirit's leading.

Spiritual-Awareness

Allow 20-25 Minutes

Every Christian is tempted to fulfill the natural desires of life in illegitimate ways on a daily basis. Some of us struggle more with sexual temptation; others with eating too much, desiring to control others, looking good at any cost, taking things that are not our property…the list could continue for pages, but you get the point.

It is surprising for some people to learn that the Bible shows us that Jesus knows what it is like to be tempted.

Hebrews 4:12-16

For the word of God is living and active. Sharper than any double-edged sword, it penetrates even to dividing soul and spirit, joints and marrow; it judges the thoughts and attitudes of the heart. Nothing in all creation is hidden from God's sight. Everything is uncovered and laid bare before the eyes of him to whom we must give account.

Therefore, since we have a great high priest who has gone through the heavens, Jesus the Son of God, let us hold firmly to the faith we profess. For we do not have a high priest who is unable to sympathize with our weaknesses, but we have one who has been tempted in every way, just as we are—yet was without sin. Let us then approach the throne of grace with confidence, so that we may receive mercy and find grace to help us in our time of need. (NASB)

What encouragement do you find from this passage?

We can know that Jesus knows, from experience, what temptation is like. Jesus is our high priest who intercedes for us with the Father. Jesus is not cold and callous to our problems but has experienced temptations himself.

The account of the wilderness temptation, which we will study in a few minutes, is a detailed exposition of what Jesus went through on one occasion, but it is important to remember that this is not *all* that he went through. The passage specifically ends with the statement that Satan left him for a while and tempted him at a more opportune time.

Surely Peter tempted Jesus when Peter advised him not to go the way of suffering (Mark 8:33). Jesus said to Peter, "Get behind Me Satan!" Jesus was also tempted in the Garden when he struggled to obey his Father's will regarding going to the cross (Luke 22:39-46). Did the woman wiping his feet with her hair also tempt Jesus? Was he tempted to multiply loaves and fishes for himself during other times of fasting? Was he tempted to judge the Pharisees during his earthly ministry instead of waiting (Matthew 23)? We cannot know the daily extent of Jesus' temptation, but we can know that he was tempted and therefore can "relate" to what we go through.

Jesus gives us a clear example of how to deal with temptation. We can learn from his example and can apply the same principles to our own situations.

Luke 4:1-15

Jesus, full of the Holy Spirit, returned from the Jordan and was led by the Spirit in the desert, where for forty days he was tempted by the devil. He ate nothing during those days, and at the end of them he was hungry.

The devil said to him, "If you are the Son of God, tell this stone to become bread."

Jesus answered, "It is written: 'Man does not live on bread alone.'"

The devil led him up to a high place and showed him in an instant all the kingdoms of the world. And he said to him, "I will give you all their authority and splendor, for it has been given to me, and I can give it to anyone I want to. So if you worship me, it will all be yours."

Jesus answered, "It is written: 'Worship the Lord your God and serve him only.'"

The devil led him to Jerusalem and had him stand on the highest point of the temple. "If you are the Son of God," he said, "throw yourself down from here. For it is written:

" 'He will command his angels concerning you to guard you carefully; they will lift you up in their hands, so that you will not strike your foot against a stone.'"

Jesus answered, "It says: 'Do not put the Lord your God to the test.'"

When the devil had finished all this tempting, he left him until an opportune time.

Jesus returned to Galilee in the power of the Spirit, and news about him spread through the whole countryside. He taught in their synagogues, and everyone praised him. (NIV)

What is the first temptation Jesus faced in this passage?

Hunger. Physical need. Make stones into bread.

Was Jesus's hunger something that was wrong in and of itself?

No, it was a normal and natural desire.

What do you think this temptation was really about?	Meeting those physical needs in an unfaithful way. Food is not wrong. Eating is not wrong. Even Jesus creating food from non-food is not wrong—see his miracle of feeding the 5,000 (Luke 9:12-17). The root of the temptation was to get Jesus to break his fast this way—to turn from God, ignore the Holy Spirit's leading, and take care of his needs himself.
How did Jesus respond?	He quoted the Scriptures.
What do you think is the meaning of the quotation?	Spiritual matters (and faithfulness) are more important than physical needs.
What is the second temptation Jesus faced in this passage?	Satan giving Jesus all the kingdoms of the world.
Would Jesus *eventually* gain these kingdoms anyway (See Psalm 110:1)?	Yes, this is another temptation to get Jesus to take something that is rightfully his but by wrong means.
What do you think this temptation is really about?	Getting Jesus to avoid the way of pain and suffering—to gain the kingdoms that are rightfully his but without going to the cross.
What would have been the *cost* of this sin?	Worship of Satan. Whenever Satan urges us to take something that is rightfully ours but by wrong means, he is encouraging us to do things his way and not God's way. To do it Satan's way is to submit to him and take him as Lord.
How did Jesus respond?	He quoted the Scriptures. He revealed the root of the temptation by showing the right form of worship.
What is the third temptation Jesus faced in this passage?	To leap from the temple and land safely.

 Facilitator's Guide: *Crossroads*, Turning Point, P. O. Box 22127, Chattanooga, TN 37422-2127

How does Satan tempt Him?	With Scripture.
What do you think this temptation really about?	Again, Jesus could have done it, and it would have been the job of the angelic host to protect him. It was not a temptation to do an overt sin, but it was a test of the Father's care. It was a call to have the Father **prove** his care for Jesus. (It would also be a marvelous miracle before the Jews and gain their praise as Messiah without the pain of the cross.)
How does Jesus respond?	He quotes other Scriptures that balance out the context of what Satan has quoted out of context.
What did Jesus's response reveal about his attitude towards the Father?	He would trust Him and not test His reliability.

 **A**pplication

Allow 20 Minutes

All the temptations Jesus faced in the wilderness focused on trying to get something without the obedience and sacrifice necessary for it.

Let's take a look at how the temptations Jesus faced relate to our struggle with temptations to indulge in sexual sin.

In the first temptation, Satan tried to prey upon a physical need (to eat) and the desire to satisfy his extreme hunger after a 40-day fast. Jesus was in the wilderness and was fasting in obedience to God's instruction. Jesus enjoyed food, but in this context he would not indulge this natural desire. He chose to live in obedience to God the Father, as he always does, which is normal. He chose not to indulge his appetite at the wrong time and in the wrong way.

How does the concept of how Jesus's refusal to indulge his hunger at the expense of obedience to the Father relate to our struggle with sexual temptation?

Sex is a normal desire. It is not evil except when it is practiced in the wrong context and for the wrong reasons. This can be compared to making bread from stones in the wrong context and for the wrong reasons. Is not a fantasy similar to making sex out of air?

The second temptation in this passage shows Satan tempting Christ with great wealth and power if only Jesus will bow down to him in worship. Satan is appealing to a deep human desire to have instant gratification. Jesus was to eventually gain these kingdoms anyway, but Satan was tempting him to take it instantly and avoid the suffering of the cross.

How does Jesus's example in declining Satan's offer of instant gratification and choosing instead the path of self-sacrifice relate to our struggle with sexual temptation?

Sex is something we can expect to find in the proper context of marriage, but to get it without going through the process of a **sacrificial** relationship is sin.

In the third temptation, Satan tempts Jesus to put God the Father to the test by jumping from the top of the temple and forcing him to protect Jesus from harm. Satan was appealing to the desire of public acclaim that is deep rooted in the human heart. Jesus would someday be worshiped as King of kings and Lord of lords but only in God's perfect timing.

How does Jesus's example of refusing Satan's temptation to force God the Father's protection and receiving public worship before the right time relate to our struggle with sexual sin?

Sex is something we have to trust God for and not demand from him—testing him. "Give it to me now or else!" His plan will be fulfilled in our lives, but we have to trust his perfect timing.

In these temptations, Jesus relied on the Scriptures to give him a proper understanding of what he was to do ("renewing the mind"), and he quoted it in times of temptation. Jesus did not take isolated verses out of context but balanced Scripture with an understanding of the true meaning of the verses.

Satan tempts us to shortcuts. Satan tempts us to fulfill physical desires and neglect spiritual ones. Satan tempts us to "do it ourselves" and not wait on God. Jesus shows us what true obedience is. Jesus, having experienced temptation, understands our condition. He is sympathetic, but He is also the perfect standard.

Yield to the will of God. Memorize Scripture. Quote it and live it. Make a specific plan of how to do this more consistently as the Lord enables you.

 Facilitator's Guide: *Crossroads,* Turning Point, P. O. Box 22127, Chattanooga, TN 37422-2127

Closing Prayer

Give thanks that Jesus understands what it is to be tempted and that he understands what we go through when Satan tempts us. Pray for the grace to respond as Jesus did, by trusting God our Father to meet our needs.

Session 11 *The Sin of Proximity*

Opening Prayer

Ask God to show group members any areas of their lives they need to change to avoid being open to temptation.

Sharing Questions

Thinking back to "The Sin System" discussed in Session 1, list some of your "rituals" leading up to your particular sexual sin.

Personal response. (The ritual may include different clothes, routes driven home, etc.)

Self-Awareness

Allow 20-25 Minutes

NOTE TO FACILITATOR:

It seems like those who struggle with sexual sin often have a hard time identifying the things they do *before* they jump into their sins. Often this lack of identification is a means of avoiding dealing with the sin of proximity—so that they can continue in their sin and make excuses for themselves. It may be helpful to have one or more of the group share specific ways they make "provision for the flesh" and what steps they have taken to correct this. (Maybe set this up ahead of time with "older" members of the group.)

Also it is important to balance the discussion in this lesson with the idea that the rules will not solve the problem. There is no "formula for success"—otherwise we would trust the formula and not God. The rules are only tools to enable us to better love Jesus. The key is to stay in fellowship with Jesus.

The sin of proximity happens when we allow ourselves to be enticed to sin by not avoiding events, people, places, objects, or anything else that we know will likely stir up lustful thoughts in our minds. Some would describe the sin of proximity as allowing ourselves to come into contact with the occasion for sin.

Every person is different, and so what may constitute an occasion for sin for one person may not be tempting or sinful for another. However, there are some things that without a doubt would be an occasion for sin for almost any healthy human being.

Make a list of things that might lead one person to sin and not affect someone else. Also list things that would almost certainly lead anyone to sin.

Reading certain books or viewing certain movies, going to dances or concerts, swimming, nonintimate physical contact, etc. might not lead some people to lustful thoughts but may totally overwhelm some others. Sexually titillating art, literature, music, dancing, intimate physical contact, or anything else designed to arouse a person sexually is almost certainly going to lead a person at the very least to sinful thoughts and perhaps even actions.

When we commit a sin of proximity, what we are doing is setting the stage for overt sin to occur. We are prone to lie to ourselves that what we are doing will not have consequences. We think we can play around the edges of sin without actually acting out the sin. This thinking is self-deceptive because sin has great power and, if entertained, will overwhelm us.

Many people who deal with sexual addictions neglect to decide before they are tempted how they are going to respond when confronted with an occasion to sin. We all have our triggers that, if pulled, will lead us to acting out our sexual impulses. We all have boundaries and points of no return that, when crossed, will unfailingly result in a loss of self-control.

Avoiding these sin traps requires decisions and actions be taken before we are confronted with the situations that tempt our weaknesses. If we can recognize these occasions for sin and learn how to avoid them, we will have greater victory against the stronghold of sin.

What are some common occasions for sin you face on a regular basis. What success have you had in avoiding these tempting situations?

Personal responses.

Spiritual Awareness Lead–In

There are occasions for sin that are totally beyond our control and seem to come out of nowhere, and there are occasions for sin that we consciously or unconsciously bring upon ourselves. Those we bring upon ourselves usually occur because we have not completely cut our relationship with our chronic sin habits.

Cutting our relationship with sinful habits requires serious choices. Romans 13:14 (NASB) instructs us to "make no provision for the flesh in regard to its lusts." The same verse in the NIV tells us to "not think about how to gratify the desires of the sinful nature."

What are some examples of how people fail to "make no provision for the flesh"?

When we find ourselves thinking about how to gratify our sinful natures, we are setting ourselves up for an occasion to sin. This thinking process is sometimes called the sin before the sin. It is very subtle and deceptive. We may go into a bookstore telling ourselves we are looking for science fiction when really we are drawn to the photography books.

Some people who say they are working to overcome sexual addictions do not destroy all their pornography, keep their unfiltered Internet access, or still drive past the old clubs and bookstores they used to frequent. They still think about satisfying the sinful urges.

Spiritual-Awareness

Allow 20-25 Minutes

God chose the Jewish people to be his own special people and entered into a covenant with them. This covenant was a special relationship where God promised to be so close that they would be his people and he would be their God. Leviticus 26:11-12 records God's words when he said, "I will put my dwelling place among you, and I will not abhor you. I will walk among you and be your God, and you will be my people" (NIV).

The Jews agreed to this special relationship and committed to live their lives in a way that pleased God. We read one of the major conditions they agreed to in Leviticus 26:1, "Do not make idols or set up an image or a sacred stone for yourselves, and do not place a carved stone in your land to bow down before it. I am the LORD your God" (NIV).

Numbers 33:50-53

> On the plains of Moab by the Jordan across from Jericho the LORD said to Moses, "Speak to the Israelites and say to them: 'When you cross the Jordan into Canaan, drive out all the inhabitants of the land before you. Destroy all their carved images and their cast idols, and demolish all their high places. Take possession of the land and settle in it, for I have given you the land to possess.' " (NIV)

Facilitator's Guide: *Crossroads*, Turning Point, P. O. Box 22127, Chattanooga, TN 37422-2127

What did God tell Moses and the people to do when entering the land?

They were to totally purge out the people and their false religions.

Why do you think He would have said these things?

God did not want the Israelites to be contaminated by false religions.

The history of the nations of Israel and Judah contains many stories of how the Jewish people failed to obey the commandment to avoid worshipping idols. Throughout their history, we read of an attraction to what were called "high places." These high places were locations where altars and shrines were set up to worship false gods.

2 Kings 17:9-12

> And the sons of Israel did things secretly which were not right, against the LORD their God. Moreover, they built for themselves high places in all their towns, from watchtower to fortified city. And they set for themselves *sacred* pillars and Asherim on every high hill and under every green tree, and there they burned incense on all the high places as the nations *did* which the LORD had carried away to exile before them; and they did evil things provoking the LORD. And they served idols, concerning which the LORD had said to them, "You shall not do this thing." (NASB)

The worship of false gods many times included sexual overtones and activities. The false god Baal wore a helmet adorned with the horns of a bull—a symbol of strength and fertility. Baal worship included ritual prostitution. Often the places displayed idols like the Asherah pole—an upright pole which some say may have represented a penis and thus symbolized fertility.

God had commanded that these places were not to be allowed to exist, yet most of the kings did not destroy them. Even the so-called *good* kings often left these places untouched. King Hezekiah is one of the few who intentionally destroyed them; but soon after his death, his son replaced them.

2 Kings 21:1-3

> Manasseh was twelve years old when he became king. . . . And he did evil in the sight of the LORD, according to the abominations of the nations whom the LORD dispossessed before the sons of Israel. For he rebuilt the high places which Hezekiah his father had destroyed; and he erected altars for Baal and made an Asherah, as Ahab king of Israel had done, and worshiped all the host of heaven and served them. (NASB)

These Old Testament accounts of God's people choosing to embrace idolatry are a major theme in the history of Israel and Judah. While some periods in their history are more encouraging than others, the temptation to worship false gods was a constant struggle—often ending in failure for the common people as well as the leaders. The leaders often did many things right but failed to deal with the idolatry that crippled their spiritual lives and prevented God's full blessing for their nations.

> Jehoash did right in the sight of the LORD all his days in which Jehoiada the priest instructed him. Only the high places were not taken away; the people still sacrificed and burned incense on the high places (2 Kings 12:2-3 NASB).

> Amaziah the son of Joash king of Judah became king. . . . Only the high places were not taken away; the people still sacrificed and burned incense on the high places (2 Kings 14:2, 4 NASB).

> And (Azariah) did right in the sight of the LORD, according to all that his father Amaziah had done. Only the high places were not taken away; the people still sacrificed and burned incense on the high places (2 Kings 15:3-4 NASB).

> And (Jotham) did what was right in the sight of the LORD; he did according to all that his father Uzziah had done. Only the high places were not taken away; the people still sacrificed and burned incense on the high places. He built the upper gate of the house of the LORD (2 Kings 15:34-35 NASB).

What could be some reasons that these kings, who were in many ways obeying God, would allow the "high places" of worship to remain?

Perhaps they were: trying to please both God and their false gods, hedging their bets against a bad day when they might need more gods than simply God, enjoying the false worship and unwilling to abandon it, avoiding the political repercussions if they alienated the false priests and worshippers.

Facilitator's Guide: *Crossroads*, Turning Point, P. O. Box 22127, Chattanooga, TN 37422-2127

What do you think was the impact of the presence of these places of idol worship on the citizens?

In your opinion, did the kings create an occasion for sin for themselves and their people? If so, did they have the ability to eliminate the influence of this occasion for sin?

Personal responses.

When it is in our power to change a situation that will likely cause us to sin and we choose not to act to change it, we are then guilty of what is called "the sin before the sin." The sin before the sin involves the little decisions we make which set us up for temptation and sin. For the kings and people of Israel and Judah, the sin before the sin was choosing not to destroy the places of false worship. The existence of these places was a constant temptation to everyone who lived during those times.

If we are to overcome the strongholds in our lives that constantly pull us in the wrong direction, we have to come to a place of radical obedience and do everything possible to eliminate those occasions for sin that are in our control. In speaking in the Sermon on the Mount, Jesus said something startling in the following verses:

Matthew 5:27-30

> You have heard that it was said, "YOU SHALL NOT COMMIT ADULTERY," but I say to you, that everyone who looks on a woman to lust for her has committed adultery with her already in his heart. And if your right eye makes you stumble, tear it out, and throw it from you; for it is better for you that one of the parts of your body perish, than for your whole body to be thrown into hell. And if your right hand makes you stumble, cut it off, and throw it from you; for it is better for you that one of the parts of your body perish, than for your whole body to go into hell. (NASB)

Why do you suppose Jesus is using such intense language here?

He is making it clear that serving God requires radical choices that go beyond simple mental assent. We are being called to a standard higher than just religious belief.

Do you think God really intends for us to literally mutilate ourselves?

Certainly not! The shocking language is used to emphasize the importance of making radical choices for obedience, not to be taken as a literal command to do ourselves physical harm.

What message do you think God is giving us through this text?

We have to be willing to do whatever it takes to deal with the sin that would dominate our lives. Radical actions are called for to prevent sin from controlling our lives and destroying us.

In the previous passage, the right eye and right hand are used to illustrate something in our lives that might *make us stumble.* This word *stumble* is a word sometimes used to describe the stick in a trap that, when moved, causes the trap to close, trapping the victim. This is not just a momentary loss of balance but a collapse that brings great danger.

Failing to take appropriate actions to eliminate the stumbling blocks in our lives that lead to sin is a serious issue for many of us.

1 Corinthians 6:18-20

> Run away from sexual sin! No other sin so clearly affects the body as this one does. For sexual immorality is a sin against your own body. Or don't you know that your body is the temple of the Holy Spirit, who lives in you and was given to you by God? You do not belong to yourself, for God bought you with a high price. So you must honor God with your body. (NLT)

We are advised to **run** from sexual sin.

Why do you believe that running away from sexual sin is good advice?

With sexual sin, the longer you are in the presence of temptation the less likely you are to escape without sinning.

In your experience, which temptation is easier to resist—the temptation to lust or the temptation to go near a situation where you can lust?

Once in the proximity of sexual temptation, the will to resist is low. "Resistance is futile!" states the Borg on Star Trek; and when we are in certain situations, it seems that way. Yet if you fight the fight on the easier terrain of the "sin before the sin," you have a significantly better chance of winning.

Facilitator's Guide: *Crossroads*, Turning Point, P. O. Box 22127, Chattanooga, TN 37422-2127

We began this Spiritual Awareness section by considering Romans 13:14. Let's look at the larger context of this verse.

Romans 13:12-14

> The night is almost gone; the day of salvation will soon be here. So don't live in darkness. Get rid of your evil deeds. Shed them like dirty clothes. Clothe yourselves with the armor of right living, as those who live in the light. We should be decent and true in everything we do, so that everyone can approve of our behavior. Don't participate in wild parties and getting drunk, or in adultery and immoral living, or in fighting and jealousy. But let the Lord Jesus Christ take control of you, and don't think of ways to indulge your evil desires. (NLT)

What are some of the actions we are called to do?

Do you think you have the strength to do these things on your own?

What is required in order to avoid even thinking of ways to indulge our evil desires?

Philippians 2:12-13

> Dearest friends, you were always so careful to follow my instructions when I was with you. And now that I am away you must be even more careful to put into action God's saving work in your lives, obeying God with deep reverence and fear. For God is working in you, giving you the desire to obey him and the power to do what pleases him. (NLT)

What do these verses tell us about how God is working in our lives?

Do not live in darkness, get rid of evil deeds like shedding dirty clothing, clothe ourselves with the armor of right living, be decent and true, avoid sinful behaviors.

No, nobody has the strength to do it alone.

The battle cannot be fought alone. We need to first put on Jesus—appeal to His mercy and grace—before we can resist even the urge to make provision for the flesh. It all circles back to Jesus, yet we need to heed his warnings to deal radically with our propensity to sin. He will give us the strength to do what He is telling us to do.

If we are paying attention to God's work in our lives, he will give us the desire and power to do what pleases him.

We have seen in this group that the Bible tells us our hearts are deceitful, so we cannot even trust ourselves. We often lie to ourselves and convince ourselves that we can do something without consequences—that we can play around the edges of our sin without actually falling into it. In our deluded thinking, we forget that sin has power that can overwhelm us when we entertain opportunities to indulge our sinful natures. We need to put into place in our lives certain practices and decisions that will deal with the sin before the sin—the sin of proximity—and give us greater victory against our sin.

When we allow ourselves to be in situations where the potential for sin is high, we are setting ourselves up to fail. The longer we stay in such a situation or entertain sinful thoughts, the stronger the potential becomes. It is much like stretching a rubber band. The tighter it is stretched, the more difficult it is to keep it from snapping back and stinging your fingers. The longer you keep it stretched, the more likely it is that it will release the potential energy stored and suddenly pop you.

Knowingly allowing ourselves to be put in situations where the potential for sin is high is foolish, yet we are tempted to do it anyway. We may surf the Internet, go cruising with no destination in mind, browse the magazines, click aimlessly through cable channels, or attend a club knowing full well that in the back of our minds we are looking for some excitement that will provide the occasion for sin. Once we put ourselves in the proximity of temptation, we are nearly committed to follow through with the sin.

Think about the last time you allowed yourself to be in a situation you knew would likely tempt you to sin.

What thoughts did you have as you entered the situation?

Personal responses.

Was there a "point of no return"?

There is usually a point when we walk toward sinning that it seems impossible to turn back.

What would you advise someone else in the same situation to do?

Personal responses.

Even more troublesome are the times when we cannot avoid a tempting situation, such as when we are alone on a business trip.

What steps can we take to make it less likely that we will lose our battle with temptation when we are in situations beyond our control?

The group by now should have many responses to this question and will probably include the following:

- Accountability to another person is extremely valuable.
- Report on a daily basis or, if necessary, several times each day to the person to whom you are accountable.
- Decide ahead of time how to respond to situations that present themselves.
- Prepare your heart before the trip. Avoid the triggers that trip you.
- Have friends pray for you and pray for yourself moment by moment, trusting God for strength and wisdom.

In Matthew 5:27-30, Jesus advises us to take drastic action against the things in our lives that cause us to sin. Of course, he does not want us to mutilate our bodies, but he does want us to be deadly serious in cutting those things out of our lives that cause us to sin.

What is the *hand* or the *eye* in your life that causes you to stumble?

Personal responses.

Has this chronic stumbling block in your battle become a *high place* in your life that you will find difficult to cast away?

Personal responses.

What is your plan for ridding your life of this hindrance to your freedom?

Personal responses.

To deal with sexual sin effectively, we must weaken the grip sin has over us by starving our sinful nature. When we "make no provision for the flesh," we are able to weaken the sin nature's power over us to feed its appetites. The "high places" of our hearts must be torn down and replaced with a devotion and moment-by-moment dependency on Jesus.

Closing Prayer

Ask God to challenge group members to remove from their lives all the false gods that threaten to pull them into sinful behaviors.

Facilitator's Guide: *Crossroads*, Turning Point, P. O. Box 22127, Chattanooga, TN 37422-2127

Session 12 Accountability

Introduction

Allow 10 Minutes

Opening Prayer

> Ask God to help members to be willing to be accountable to at least one person.

Sharing Questions

> Try to find out if members have an adequate support system that holds them accountable.

Who holds you accountable for your actions at work and leisure?

> Personal responses.

Where do you need more accountability?

> Personal responses.

Self-Awareness

Allow 20-25 Minutes

> NOTE TO FACILITATOR:
>
> This would be a good meeting to check with the members to see if they have accountability partners and how they work together. How often do they check in with their accountability partner? Do they have more than one in case one is unavailable in a crisis?
>
> If individuals are struggling with homosexual temptations, it is best they have phone accountability with each other. Another option may be to link up one who struggles with homosexual temptations with one who struggles with heterosexual temptations. This way, the accountability relationship cannot be twisted by the flesh into an opportunity to sin. Accountability is so critical to breaking the power of sexual sin that it is important for the facilitator make every effort to see that each person has an accountability partner.

Light exists but darkness does not because darkness has no substance of its own. Darkness is simply the absence of light. Outer space is dark because in the vast emptiness there is nothing to reflect the light. A shadow is dark because something is blocking the light. When light pierces into darkness, what is concealed is suddenly revealed. A single match can light the deepest, darkest night. John 1:5 states, "And the light shines in the darkness, and the darkness did not overpower it."

No matter how small the light, it still drives back the darkness because darkness has no strength against light.

The power of darkness comes in its ability to conceal reality. A dark room may be filled with gold, but it is not visible without light. The same room might be filled with bones, but they are not visible without the light. How many times have youngsters at a youth camp stuck their hands into a bowl of spaghetti in the dark, being told it was a bowl of worms and believed it?

The power of secret sin is similar to the power of darkness. Secret sin attempts to conceal something that is detestable in the shadows of darkness. Sinful deeds done in secret take their enslaving power from the very fact that they are in the darkness, concealed, and not dealt with. So long as they are secret, the person involved in them neither seeks nor receives help because nobody is aware of what is happening. Secrecy keeps the sin hidden from possible intervention.

Consider the words of Proverbs 7:8-10.

> Passing along the street near her corner;
> And he took the path to her house
> In the twilight, in the evening,
> In the black and dark night.
> And there a woman met him,
> With the attire of a harlot, and a crafty heart. (NKJV)

What words are used to describe the time and circumstance of this encounter with the harlot?

Twilight, evening, black and dark night.

Do you think the words *secrecy* and *darkness* are good descriptions of the physical and spiritual environments where sexual sin is encouraged?

Personal responses.

Why or why not?

The physical environments of strip clubs, adult movie houses, etc., are often very dimly lit. Sinful activity is often carried on in dimly lit areas, behind closed doors, and in remote locations to preserve secrecy.

The power of secret sin is that it can deceive the person engaged in it into thinking it is not as bad as it is—that it is not as enslaving as it really is. On the other hand, another power of secret sin is that someone might think it is worse than it really is and give up hope. The strength of secret sin is that without outside help, the person can be totally deceived, entangled, and enslaved.

Facilitator's Guide: *Crossroads*, Turning Point, P. O. Box 22127, Chattanooga, TN 37422-2127

Some people live for years with dark shadows in their lives that cover secret areas where sinful behaviors have ensnared them. The one thing they dread is being exposed, but it is exposure to the light that can bring them freedom from self-destructive choices.

What has been your experience with having a *dark area* in your life?

Personal responses.

When was it exposed to the light?

Personal responses.

How did it happen?

Personal responses.

Once the light has exposed the secret areas of our lives, then we can receive the help we need to overcome what is enslaving us. We can receive help from others who have walked through the obstacles we are sure to encounter. We all need helpers to advise and warn us and hold us accountable to walking in the light.

Because so much of sexual sin is a complex web of temptations—many rooted in the sins of the fathers—a guide is essential to helping someone see what is going on. The *objective* helper can see the patterns and the life issues, which the enslaved person cannot see.

God gives us three means of grace to overcome sinful habits: (1) his Word, (2) his Spirit, and (3) his people—fellow Christians. We need other believers to *speak the truth in love* and help us in our struggles with sin.

Spiritual Awareness Lead–In

Secret sin by definition is hidden from people in our lives who would hold us accountable for our actions. It is relatively easy for a person to harbor secret sin and to make it part of his or her lifestyle. Because this is true, the old saying that "what others don't know can't hurt us" seems to make a lot of sense.

We may be able to hide our thoughts and actions from other people, but one thing we need to consider is that nothing is hidden from God and that someday even our secret motives will be revealed.

> So be careful not to jump to conclusions before the Lord returns as to whether or not someone is faithful. When the Lord comes, he will bring our deepest secrets to light and will reveal our private motives. And then God will give to everyone whatever praise is due (1 Corinthians 4:5 NLT).

Have you ever imagined what it would be like to be free of the hidden area(s) of your life? What difference do you think it would make in your feelings about yourself if this were to happen? (Or if it has already, what difference did you experience?)

Personal responses.

Spiritual-Awareness

Allow 20-25 Minutes

The Bible often contrasts darkness to light and encourages us to live in the light and forsake the darkness.

Ephesians 5:3-16

> But immorality or any impurity or greed must not even be named among you, as is proper among saints; and *there must be no* filthiness and silly talk, or coarse jesting, which are not fitting, but rather giving of thanks. For this you know with certainty, that no immoral or impure person or covetous man, who is an idolater, has an inheritance in the kingdom of Christ and God. Let no one deceive you with empty words, for because of these things the wrath of God comes upon the sons of disobedience. Therefore do not be partakers with them; for you were formerly darkness, but now you are light in the Lord; walk as children of light (for the fruit of the light *consists* in all goodness and righteousness and truth), trying to learn what is pleasing to the Lord. And do not participate in the unfruitful deeds of darkness, but instead even expose them; for it is disgraceful even to speak of the things which are done by them in secret. But all things become visible when they are exposed by the light, for everything that becomes visible is light. For this reason it says, "Awake, sleeper, and arise from the dead, and Christ will shine on you." Therefore be careful how you walk, not as unwise men, but as wise, making the most of your time, because the days are evil. (NASB)

Which actions are described as belonging to the darkness?

Darkness: immorality, impurity, greed, filthiness, silly talk, coarse jesting.

Which belong to the light?

Light: goodness, righteousness, truth, learning to please God, exposing the darkness.

How are we to respond to these two groups of actions?

We respond by not being deceived by empty words that would excuse sinful behaviors, and we learn to be careful in how we walk (our actions).

Facilitator's Guide: *Crossroads*, Turning Point, P. O. Box 22127, Chattanooga, TN 37422-2127

This passage contradicts the attitudes and values that rule our culture today and excuse all types of sexual impurity. For people who are struggling with sexual sin, reading this passage is uncomfortable, but that is the function of the light of God's Word. Sometimes it is so bright it makes us cringe. Even though it may hurt, the intent is not to harm but to heal our brokenness.

Although we may sometimes be comforted by dark places when our hearts are not following the Lord, we are never hidden from God as is related in Psalm 139:7-12.

> I can never escape from your spirit. I can never get away from your presence!
>
> If I go up to heaven, you are there; if I go down to the place of the dead, you are there.
>
> If I ride the wings of the morning, if I dwell by the farthest oceans, even there your hand will guide me, and your strength will support me.
>
> I could ask the darkness to hide me and the light around me to become night— but even in darkness I cannot hide from you. To you the night shines as bright as day. Darkness and light are both alike to you. (NLT)

Psalm 139 was not written by someone trying to hide from God but by someone who was comforted by the fact that he could never escape God's presence. Nevertheless, it applies to our discussion of the futility of trying to use the darkness to hide from God.

How much of your sexual sin is secret? To what extent are your family and friends aware of this problem?

Answers may vary, but most likely a significant portion of the sin has been kept secret. It is likely that some or all of it has recently been brought into the light or the individual would probably not be in the group seeking help.

How much of the dynamic leading up to your sin is secret (i.e., lustful gazing at the office or mall before you start after more overt means of stimulation, sneaking a look at porn, sneaking into an adult place)?

Again, answers may vary, but try to reveal the pattern of secrecy leading to secret sins.

When we have secret areas in our lives where we harbor sinful thoughts, attitudes, and behaviors, we are drained of any spiritual power we might otherwise have. This is because we know the things we are doing are not pleasing to God. We live in fear because we all know instinctively the words we find in Hebrews 4:13.

> Nothing in all creation can hide from him. Everything is naked and exposed before his eyes. This is the God to whom we must explain all that we have done. (NLT)

Even though we cannot hide from God, we still try to hide from our peers who would disapprove of our lifestyle choices. We live a secret life.

Describe the power this secrecy holds over us.

People who have secret sins often think that if people knew what they were doing in secret, they would be repulsed. "If he really knew me, he would hate me," accuses the inner voice.

In what way do you see shame linked to this?

In *The Sin System,* shame leads back to preoccupation and keeps the sin pattern going. We keep our sins secret because we are ashamed and do not want to be exposed, but the secrecy enables repeated sins and therefore more shame.

An accountability partner will not be shocked by our disclosure and will help break the secrecy/shame dynamic.

Shame grips us when we think that if anyone finds out what we are really doing, they would reject us. Since deep down we know that God knows us already, we are ashamed to face him as well.

It is difficult for us to balance these two truths in our minds, but even though God holds us accountable for our choices, he never stops loving us and is willing to restore us if we will admit to our failure and confess our sin. It is when we deny and excuse our sin that we are alienated from His grace.

1 John 1:5-2:2

> This is the message he has given us to announce to you: God is light and there is no darkness in him at all. So we are lying if we say we have fellowship with God but go on living in spiritual darkness. We are not living in the truth. But if we are living in the light of God's presence, just as Christ is, then we have fellowship with each other, and the blood of Jesus, his Son, cleanses us from every sin.
>
> If we say we have no sin, we are only fooling ourselves and refusing to accept the truth. But if we confess our sins to him, he is faithful and just to forgive us and to cleanse us from every wrong. If we claim we have not sinned, we are calling God a liar and showing that his word has no place in our hearts.
>
> My dear children, I am writing this to you so that you will not sin. But if you do sin, there is someone to plead for you before the Father. He is Jesus Christ, the one who pleases God completely. He is the sacrifice for our sins. He takes away not only our sins but the sins of all the world. (NLT)

What practical steps do you find in this passage that will ensure that you continue to live in the light, even after making choices that do not please God?

We never hide, excuse, or deny our sins; we confess our sins; we trust God to forgive our sins because of Christ's sacrifice for our sins. If we do these things, we find forgiveness and walk in the light.

Not only are we instructed to confess our sins to God, but the Bible also tells us there is great healing power in confessing our sins to one another.

James 5:16

> Therefore, confess your sins to one another, and pray for one another, so that you may be healed. The effective prayer of a righteous man can accomplish much. (NASB)

Why might you be reluctant to confess your sins to another person?

Likely responses will include feeling ashamed, fear of exposure, not trusting the person to keep confidence, fear of being judged, etc.

Galatians 6:1-3

> Brethren, even if a man is caught in any trespass, you who are spiritual, restore such a one in a spirit of gentleness; *each one* looking to yourself, lest you too be tempted. Bear one another's burdens, and thus fulfill the law of Christ. For if anyone thinks he is something when he is nothing, he deceives himself. (NASB)

What should be our attitude when dealing with one another when we lapse into sin?

Gentleness, humility, willing to restore, knowing that any of us could be in the same situation.

Application

Allow 20 Minutes

In the New Testament we are taught to confront our sins and failures directly and honestly, exposing our lives to the light of God's Word, God's Spirit and God's people.

It is tempting to try to justify our sinful behaviors by "explaining away" the plain meaning of God's Word. If we do this, we are only deceiving ourselves and walking once again into the darkness. If we are sinning in the darkness of secrecy, the light of God's Word needs to shine brighter into our lives.

What practical steps can you describe that we can take to bring the light of God's Word more intensely into our lives?

The most important is to read, study, and listen to, meditate upon, memorize, and interact in all possible ways to great quantities of the Scriptures.

When we sin in secrecy, we also must deceive ourselves into believing that we are hiding our actions from God. Although this is impossible, because God is everywhere and knows all things, most of us find ways to pretend that God cannot see our actions or else convince ourselves that he really does not care what we do.

What practical steps can you suggest that will help you to realize that God's Spirit is aware of every aspect of your life, even your secret motives?

There may be many suggestions here, but they will all come down to methods of living in a moment-by-moment conversation with God as we go through our days.

All of the means of grace that God provides us to overcome sinful behaviors are equally important, but one of the most neglected ones is choosing to be personally accountable to one or more fellow believers for our actions. There are many reasons for this, but the most common one is fear of exposure. In order for us to feel safe in confiding in another believer, we have to be able to trust the people to whom we make ourselves vulnerable.

Here are some guidelines to help in finding an accountability partner.

• Be careful not to share your struggles with just anyone—someone who is either careless or malicious could betray your confidence. Find a mature believer who is emotionally and spiritually stable.

• Accountability partners should be "safe" people, that is, people who will not be tempted and will not tempt us sexually.

• Accountability partners should be willing to be open about their struggles.

• Be careful in how you disclose your failures to your accountability partner. Do not be graphic—if you have looked at pornography, admit it but do not describe the details of what you viewed. If you had intercourse, admit it but do not describe the details.

• Your accountability partner should not excuse you nor condemn you, just listen to you. Your accountability partner should listen to you; pray for you; ask you how you are doing in your struggles with sin; point out your attempts to minimize, rationalize, or hide your sin; and encourage you to grow closer to Christ.

• Your accountability partner should be someone other than your spouse. Making your spouse into an accountability partner puts him or her too much into the role of a *cop* and will create a destructive dynamic in your relationship. The shaming which can occur in this situation feeds the sin system, and you will be tempted to sin all the more. Accountability needs to be to someone who can help you determine when or if something needs to be confessed to your spouse. (It is critical to distinguish between temptations, the sin of lustful looking, the sin of lustful masturbation and/or an adulterous sexual contact. If informed about every temptation, lustful thought, or look, your spouse would be overwhelmed.)

- Always confess to the Lord and to your accountability partner. Ask God for wisdom about confessing to your spouse. Such confessions may make you feel better, but dumping everything on your spouse can be overwhelming and damage or destroy your relationship.

It can be intimidating at first, but it is no accident that God instructs us to be mutually accountable. See this as a means of strengthening your commitment to God—it is not being a man-pleaser to have accountability. It is out of a commitment to God and His methods that you do this. Your accountability person *enables* you to better honor God. Pray that the Lord will lead you to that person and that you will begin to have accountability.

An accountability partner is someone you can talk to *before* temptations become sins. Temptations often lose their power once they are brought into the light—they are revealed to be absurd. They often seem ridiculous once articulated, and the other person can give you specific advice and encouragement.

An accountability partner can also help you see through the haze of shame and encourage you not to cycle back into preoccupation. This is often done by speaking gospel promises to you. Not all accountability involves confrontation—much of it is encouragement.

How do you see accountability helping you to break the power of sin in your life?

You are not fighting alone. Others are praying, and others are asking about how you are doing. Others can also see clearly when you cannot. The power of secrecy and shame are broken.

Write down the name(s) of some people whom you plan to ask to keep you accountable. Make a plan to ask them this week.

Closing Prayer

Pray that fear or shame will not prevent members from forming accountable relationships. Ask God to bring the right person along to be the "safe" accountability partner for each member.

Facilitator's Guide: *Crossroads,* Turning Point, P. O. Box 22127, Chattanooga, TN 37422-2127

Session **13** *Perseverance*

Introduction

Opening Prayer

Give thanks for each member who has completed the group sessions thus far.

Sharing Questions

How is the process of accountability helping you deal with temptation and sin?

Personal responses.

Self-Awareness

Allow 20-25 Minutes

NOTE TO FACILITATOR:

The subject of persevering in the faith is important because people are often so full of shame and self-defeat they cannot get out of the sin cycle. Since proper guilt performs the critical function of bringing us to confession, we must be careful not to harden our hearts to a sense of the wrongness of our acts and thoughts. Hardening of the heart is what sank most of us into the deeper depravities we are involved with—one sin led to another and to another. We cannot simply "accept ourselves" at the risk of continuing in our sin. Yet without discerning between proper guilt and improper shame, we will end up stuck in the cycle. It is very important, therefore, that we are able to discern between guilt and shame. We need to be able to see how one leads to repentance and the other to despair. It does not hurt to belabor this distinction in the discussion time.

There are many places in the sin system where God intervenes to break us out of the bondage. We have looked at several of these spots throughout these weeks. One of the most crucial spots in the cycle is yet to be discussed—the guilt and shame location. This is how we feel and how we think *after* we commit our sin. (It may even be how we feel after we are merely tempted and are confronted by our inner wants and desires, even if we do not sin through action.) Guilt and shame are two very common feelings we have.

Many people have discovered that the guilt and shame portion of the sin system is the most potent in keeping a person trapped in sexual sin. When guilt and feelings of shame are not dealt with in a healthy and biblical manner, most people will plunge right back into the cycle of sin called sexual addiction. This process involves the dynamic of preoccupation and the need to find a way to cope with the weight of the shame and guilt. Preoccupation causes people to think about the very things they are ashamed of, and the remembrance creates a desire to experience them again. The self-destructive thoughts and behaviors that are hated so much continue to lure the person to make sinful choices.

One common lie of preoccupied thought is: "I can't believe I did that. That was disgusting. That was wrong. That sort of felt good though. Maybe it isn't all that bad. Well, it sure would make me feel better than I feel now."

Another aspect of this is that when the guilt and shame are unresolved in a biblical way, they can be used as reasons to sin again. Satan may say, "Look at how sinful you are. God can't forgive you. Since you can't be forgiven, you might as well enjoy it again."

A third aspect, which again is subtle, is that when the guilt and shame are not resolved—when the person still feels guilty and ashamed even after confession—then Satan can encourage the person to take care of the pain in another way. If God is not going to take care of the pain, then the person reasons that the pain can be handled without God's help. The result is to decide to "self-medicate" by repeating the sin.

Which of the above three dynamics of preoccupation is most common in your experience?

Personal responses.

All three of these attacks are based on a misrepresentation of biblical grace. We are open to these attacks when we do not understand the role of the Holy Spirit in repentance. There is a proper form of guilt—the awareness that certain thoughts, words, and deeds are sinful. Yet when that guilt is blurred and blended into shame, it does not bring about the purposes of God. Guilt is to bring us to repentance. Shame cannot do that. Shame is a way of thinking and living—it sees personal worth as defined by actions and abilities. Guilt says, "What I did was horrible." Shame says, "I am horrible."

How perceptive do you believe yourself to be in distinguishing between actual guilt and feelings of shame in your life experience?

Personal responses.

Facilitator's Guide: *Crossroads,* Turning Point, P. O. Box 22127, Chattanooga, TN 37422-2127

Outside of Christ, we are worthy of God's just punishment; but if a person is in a saving relationship with God, then that person is a new creation. And that new creation is not horribly defective; he or she is a masterpiece of God's grace.

Satan uses shame to continue to pile a sense of guilt on us even after we have repented. He does this in order to get us to doubt our forgiveness. Satan continues to accuse falsely so as to destroy faith and lure us back to sin.

Spiritual Awareness Lead–In

As people, it is only natural to think of God through the filter of our own human limitations. Our limitations make it impossible to love and forgive as God loves and forgives. His capacity to love all of humanity and offer forgiveness to those who turn to him is infinite. When we imagine ourselves in God's place, almost every one of us would have lost hope and patience with the human race long ago.

We must persevere in our battles with our fallen human natures even when we fail God, ourselves and those we love. God's love and acceptance of us is not dependent upon our perfect obedience. To experience this love and acceptance, we need to turn to Him in brokenness and repentance.

Israel's King David was known as "a person after God's own heart." He had many failures in his life and wrote the following words after one of his most terrible sins was exposed.

Psalm 51:16-17

Read together as a group.

> You would not be pleased with sacrifices, or I would bring them. If I brought you a burnt offering, you would not accept it.

> The sacrifice you want is a broken spirit. A broken and repentant heart, O God, you will not despise. (NLT)

Typically, what is your state of mind after experiencing a defeat in your struggle against sin?

Personal responses.

Are you tempted to believe that God has given up on you?

Personal responses.

What hope can you find from David's words in Psalm 51?

Personal responses.

Let's review "The Sin System" and its major components found on page 10.

Draw on a board the sin system diagram (page 10) and discuss each part briefly in review.

How do you think guilt and shame work together to drive us deeper into sin and despair?

The guilt and shame keep us thinking about the sin, and this leads back to preoccupation. There are also several lies of Satan which are standard at this point, including, "Well, you are already so deep into your sin you might as well do it again," or "God won't forgive me again, so I have no real hope and might as well just enjoy what little I have." Satan also lures individuals to "medicate" their shame/pain with the "drug" of more sin.

How do you define shame? How does growing up in a shame-based family create a way of thinking which is not biblical.

Describe how a parent might shame a child instead of distinguishing the difference between sin and personal value as a creation of God, etc. Describe how shame says, "I am not worthy." Describe how shame encourages us to be the "slime" we think we are. [Example: A parent can tell a child he did a wrong thing and needs to apologize and make amends, or a parent can tell a child he is "no good and will never amount to anything" because he did a wrong thing. The second is shaming.]

Read 2 Corinthians 7:10.

> For God can use sorrow in our lives to help us turn away from sin and seek salvation. We will never regret that kind of sorrow. But sorrow without repentance is the kind that results in death. (NLT)

How does God use our sense of guilt to bring us to repentance?

Only those who feel guilt will turn from their sins. You do not turn from that which you think is acceptable and right.

Is it enough for us just to be sorry for our sins, or is something else necessary?

We must move beyond feeling guilt and sorrow for our sins to repentance.

Hebrews 4:12-13

> For the word of God is living and active. Sharper than any double-edged sword, it penetrates even to dividing soul and spirit, joints and marrow; it judges the thoughts and attitudes of the heart. Nothing in all creation is hidden from God's sight. Everything is uncovered and laid bare before the eyes of him to whom we must give account. (NIV)

What is the role of the Bible and the Holy Spirit in this process of repentance?

The Holy Spirit uses the Word of God to "cut us to the bone" and bring us to an awareness of our desperate need for forgiveness in Christ.

Read together as a group.

Psalm 51:1-7

For the choir director: A psalm of David, regarding the time Nathan the prophet came to him after David had committed adultery with Bathsheba.

Have mercy on me, O God, because of your unfailing love. Because of your great compassion, blot out the stain of my sins.

Wash me clean from my guilt. Purify me from my sin.

For I recognize my shameful deeds—they haunt me day and night.

Against you, and you alone, have I sinned; I have done what is evil in your sight. You will be proved right in what you say, and your judgment against me is just.

For I was born a sinner—yes, from the moment my mother conceived me.

But you desire honesty from the heart, so you can teach me to be wise in my inmost being.

Purify me from my sins, and I will be clean; wash me, and I will be whiter than snow. (NLT)

Do you see any indication in this psalm that David moves beyond feeling guilty and goes on to repentance?

He admits he is wrong and makes no excuses for his failure. He totally agrees with God and does not justify himself. He sees the importance of honesty and opens himself to God's instruction.

Is there any evidence in this psalm that David did not allow his feelings of shame to convince him that his situation was hopeless?

In verse 3, he is clearly describing his actions as being shameful. He feels guilty for what he has done, but he still has enough confidence in God's grace that he does not count himself as worthless in God's eyes. In verse 5, he recognizes his sinful condition; however, in verse 6, he knows God values him enough to desire to instruct him.

Application

Allow 20 Minutes

If we are to grow in our spiritual lives, we will have to be able to discern the difference between the Holy Spirit's voice and and the voice of the enemy. The Holy Spirit brings conviction to our hearts for our sins. The enemy brings condemnation to our hearts and tempts us to revert to a shame-based pattern of thinking about ourselves.

The Holy Spirit in love lets us feel an appropriate level of guilt. While it may be painful, it is designed to bring us to our senses and motivate us to stop our sin and return to fellowship with God our Father.

The enemy, out of hatred for God and his people, seeks to drive us to despair and tells us lies such as, "You are not worth God's time," or "There is no hope for you." God brings guilt to motivate us to change; Satan brings shame to push us further into disobedience and despair.

The enemy also tries to keep us feeling guilty even after we have honestly confessed our sins and God has forgiven them. This is why it is common for us to want to pay for our sins by punishing ourselves. We think that because we still feel guilty, the sacrifice of Christ for our sins was not sufficient.

Let's read 1 John 1:9.

> If we confess our sins, he is faithful and just and will forgive us our sins and purify us from all unrighteousness. (NIV)

If we repent and confess our sins, what assurance do we have?

We are forgiven in Christ.

If we continue to feel guilt and shame after we have confessed, what is happening?

It is possible you may still be clinging to your sin—that you did not truly repent of it. It is more likely that you are experiencing an attack of the enemy.

Facilitator's Guide: *Crossroads*, Turning Point, P. O. Box 22127, Chattanooga, TN 37422-2127

This is where we must persevere and patiently follow Jesus—refusing to be distracted by the noise around us—focusing on the goal.

Let's read Hebrews 12:1-13.

Therefore, since we are surrounded by such a huge crowd of witnesses to the life of faith, let us strip off every weight that slows us down, especially the sin that so easily hinders our progress. And let us run with endurance the race that God has set before us. We do this by keeping our eyes on Jesus, on whom our faith depends from start to finish. He was willing to die a shameful death on the cross because of the joy he knew would be his afterward. Now he is seated in the place of highest honor beside God's throne in heaven. Think about all he endured when sinful people did such terrible things to him, so that you don't become weary and give up. After all, you have not yet given your lives in your struggle against sin.

And have you entirely forgotten the encouraging words God spoke to you, his children? He said,

"My child, don't ignore it when the Lord disciplines you, and don't be discouraged when he corrects you. For the Lord disciplines those he loves, and he punishes those he accepts as his children."

As you endure this divine discipline, remember that God is treating you as his own children. Whoever heard of a child who was never disciplined? If God doesn't discipline you as he does all of his children, it means that you are illegitimate and are not really his children after all. Since we respect our earthly fathers who disciplined us, should we not all the more cheerfully submit to the discipline of our heavenly Father and live forever?

For our earthly fathers disciplined us for a few years, doing the best they knew how. But God's discipline is always right and good for us because it means we will share in his holiness. No discipline is enjoyable while it is happening—it is painful! But afterward there will be a quiet harvest of right living for those who are trained in this way.

So take a new grip with your tired hands and stand firm on your shaky legs. Mark out a straight path for your feet. Then those who follow you, though they are weak and lame, will not stumble and fall but will become strong. (NLT)

What are some spiritual principles given in this passage that we can live by in our journey to freedom from sexual addiction.

We can expect to experience discipline from God when we sin, yet we need to persevere and not give up. The Holy Spirit brings the pain of guilt to lead us to repentance. (Satan will try to capitalize on this and create shame so that it leads to despair and not repentance.) The key is persevering. Perseverance actually produces the strength needed to persevere (Hebrews 12:13). Other verses that point to this process are James 1:2-4 and 2 Peter 1:5-7.

Part of the process of perseverance is continuing in a group that will challenge you to continue on the road to sexual purity. Some may want to repeat this study. Others may go on to other groups. Turning Point Ministries has several groups you will find helpful, such as the *Insight Group, Stepping Into Freedom,* or *Completely Free!*

Closing Prayer

Allow members to pray for one another, asking for wisdom that each person will follow God's will and pursue him with all his/her heart.

Selected Bibliography

Arterburn, Stephen. *Addicted to Love*. Ann Arbor, Michigan: Servant Publications, 1991.

Bridges, Jerry. *Transforming Grace*. Colorado Springs: Navpress, 1993.

Carnes, Patrick. *Out of the Shadows*. 2nd Edition. Center City, MI: Hazelden, 1992.

_____. *Contrary to Love*. Center City, MI: Hazelden, 1989.

_____. *Don't Call It Love*. New York: Bantam Books, 1991.

Crabb, Larry. *The Silence of Adam*. Grand Rapids: Zondervan, 1995.

Edwards, Jonathan. *Freedom of the Will*. New York: Irvington Publishing Inc., 1982.

Leahy, Frederick S. *Satan Cast Out*. Edinburgh: The Banner of Truth Trust, 1975.

Gerstner, John H. *A Primer on Free Will*. Phillipsburg, PA: P & R Publishing, 1982.

Lewis, C. S. *The Screwtape Letters*. New York: Macmillan Publishing Company, 1942.

Longacre, David E. "Teens, Porn & Solo Sex." *Harvest News*, Spring 2000, pp 1-4.

Lundgaard, Chris. *The Enemy Within*. Phillipsburg, PA: P & R Publishing, 1998.

Medinger, Alan P. "Is Masturbation Always a Sin?" *The Journal of Biblical Counseling*, Vol. 15, No. 1, Fall 1996, pp. 65-66.

Powlison, David. *Power Encounters: Reclaiming Spiritual Warfare*. Grand Rapids: Baker Books, 1995.

Rabinowitz, Craig. "His Question: 'How and why could I do this?' " *Philadelphia Inquirer*, Friday, October 31, 1997, p. A20.

Schaumburg, Dr. Harry W. *False Intimacy*. Colorado Springs: Navpress, 1997.

White, John. *Eros Defiled*. Downers Grove, Illinois: IVP, 1977.